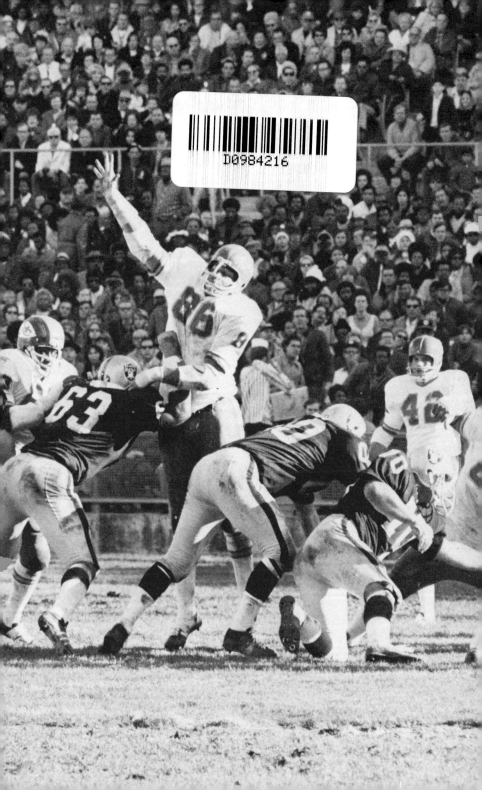

GAMEBREAKERS
OF THE NFL

Exciting profiles of seven NFL stars who can turn defeat into victory for their teams. Included are Alan Page, George Blanda, Larry Little, Jim Plunkett, Jan Stenerud, Bruce Taylor and Willie Lanier.

GAMEBREAKERS
OF THE NFL

by Bill Gutman

illustrated with photographs

Random House · New York

Copyright © 1973 by Random House, Inc.
All rights reserved under International and Pan-American Copyright Conventions.
Published in the United States by Random House, Inc., New York, and simultaneously in Canada by Random House of Canada Limited, Toronto.
Published under license from National Football League Properties, Inc.
Manufactured in the United States of America

Library of Congress Cataloging in Publication Data
Gutman, Bill.   Gamebreakers of the NFL.
(Punt, pass & kick library)
SUMMARY: Profiles of seven notable football players of the NFL: Alan Page, George Blanda, Larry Little, Jim Plunkett, Jan Stenerud, Bruce Taylor, Willie Lanier.
1. Football—Biography—Juvenile literature.
2. National Football League.   [1. Football—Biography.
2. National Football League]   I. Title.
GV939.A1G87 1973   796.33′2′0922 [920]   73-4234
ISBN 0-394-82501-2   ISBN 0-394-92501-7 (lib. bdg.)

In memory of my father,
George Gutman

The author would like to thank Joe Browne and Kay O'Reilly of the National Football League office, and the publicity departments of all teams represented for their help in obtaining background material for this book.

Contents

Introduction

Football is truly a team game. It takes a well-balanced, 40-man squad to win a championship. To succeed over the long competitive season, a club must be solid both offensively and defensively, and it must be rich in specialty-team talent.

In its most exciting moments, however, football is something more than a team game. There are some players who have the rare ability to rise above team play. The really great ones can take charge and single-handedly change the course of action when their teams need an extra push. We call these men gamebreakers because any time they step onto the field they can break the game wide open.

Great gamebreakers can be found anywhere on a team. They may be quarterbacks, fullbacks, receivers, linebackers, cornerbacks, or tackles . . . yes, even place-kickers. But no matter what position they play, these individuals all have one thing in common: a special talent that makes them capable of turning a game completely around. With their unique brand of magic, nothing seems impossible.

Gamebreakers of the NFL tells the dramatic stories of seven such stars. They are all men with a special something that makes them winners. These are the standouts in the game, players whose deeds have made gridiron history.

GAMEBREAKERS
OF THE NFL

1

Alan Page

One afternoon in December of 1971, Alan Page got mad.

The Minnesota Vikings were playing the Detroit Lions in an important late-season game. The Vikings were leading 14–3 midway through the second period, but the Lions had begun showing signs of life.

Alan Page lined up at his defensive tackle position. At 6-foot-4 and 245 pounds, Page was one of the quickest tackles in the league. "He gets into the opposing backfield before the ball does," a quarterback once said. But on this play the referee didn't like the way Page got into the opposing backfield. He called Alan for a personal foul, and the ball advanced 15 yards toward the Minnesota goal line.

On the next play Page charged Lion quarterback Greg Landry, hitting him just after he threw the ball. Again the flag went down. Again Page was called, this time for roughing the passer. The second straight penalty gave the Lions a first down in Minnesota territory.

Page was furious. He stomped up and down, shouted at the ref and glared at the Detroit huddle. In the next few minutes, Alan Page would show everyone just how a defensive tackle could be a gamebreaker.

The Lions came up to the line. If they could score, they could catch up on the Vikings and perhaps turn the game in their own favor. But at the snap, Alan Page brushed aside an offensive lineman, ran over a blocking back and headed straight for Landry. The Lion quarterback wanted to pass, but Page grabbed him and slammed him to the ground. Loss of nine.

On the next play, Page charged again. This time he was double-teamed, but he drove until one of the blockers held him in desperation. The holding penalty pushed the Lions back another 15 yards.

Still second down. Landry dropped back to pass. He looked for his receiver. Then, out of the corner of his eye he saw Page. Big number 88 had run over his blocker and was after the passer. Landry threw hurriedly, then ducked. The pass was incomplete, but a Viking penalty kept the down the same.

14

Alan Page brings down a quarterback, the Cowboys' Roger Staubach.

Another snap. Landry dropped back once more. Suddenly there was Page again, charging like a wild bull. Landry went down for another loss of nine.

Now on third and long yardage, Landry tried a draw play, hoping to catch the Vikings off guard. He dropped back but then gave the ball to halfback Altie Taylor. But before Taylor could take a step, he was buried under 245 pounds of Alan Page.

Page had pushed the Lions back 33 yards in one series of downs. Their punt on fourth down was partially blocked. Page himself later blocked a punt that led to a safety and spent the remainder of the game in the Lion backfield. The Vikings went on to an easy 29–10 victory.

"Alan was just showing some of his potential," said Viking coach Bud Grant after the game. "It shows you what he's capable of doing. Sometimes his power is frightening. He just got a little upset when those two penalties were called."

All Lion coach Joe Schmidt could say was, "When Page wants to come, he comes."

Alan Page had been making life miserable for quarterbacks and runners since 1967, when he was named NFL Defensive Rookie of the Year. His personal blitz of the Lions wasn't an isolated incident. Throughout his career he was a menace to offensive units everywhere. He punished and harassed, chased and hounded, hit and dropped the best of them. In 1971, shortly after their win over the Lions, the Vikings clinched their fourth consecutive Central Division championship. And Alan Page became the first defensive player in the history of the NFL to be named the league's Most Valuable Player.

"I think you'd have to say that Alan Page is as great as any defensive player who has ever played this game," commented coach Grant.

Then Grant ticked off some of Alan's statistics for the 1971 season. Numbers can't tell the whole story, but they begin to describe Page's fantastic season. Alan was credited with 109 solo tackles in 14 games, including ten tackles of opposing quarterbacks behind the line of scrimmage. Two of his tackles were in the opponent's end zone, scoring safeties for Minnesota. Page recovered three fumbles deep in enemy territory and blocked one point-after-touchdown kick.

Another statistic kept by the Vikings was called a "hurry," which was recorded whenever a player forced an opposing quarterback to throw the ball before he was ready or before the receiver was open. In 1971, Alan Page had 42 "hurries."

"Alan more than deserved the MVP award," Grant concluded. "He's the personification of a football player who sees the opportunity to make a big play, then has the ability to carry through and make it. It's not a coincidence that he's the one who recovers the key fumbles and makes the big plays."

As for Alan, he was characteristically modest and reserved. Upon accepting the prize, he said simply, "I'm surprised and honored. Now all I can do is try to keep improving."

Alan was born in Canton, Ohio, and his family lived in the middle of the industrial city. Mr. Page was a hard-working man who owned a juke-box distributor business and later a bar. When Alan was in the fourth grade, the Pages realized a long-time ambition by moving to the suburb of East Canton.

When Alan was 14, his mother died suddenly. Even after this tragedy, Alan remained a quiet, easygoing youngster. His only connection with violence was his football career, which had begun in junior high school. By the time he reached Canton Central Catholic High, he was already on his way to becoming a star.

As a junior, Alan was well over 200 pounds and still growing. And he ran over his high school opponents as if they were still in the Pee Wee League. In his senior year, scholarship offers began to pour in from major powers in college football.

"I don't even know how many offers I got," he recalled, "but I picked Notre Dame and the choice wasn't very difficult for me."

Notre Dame's coach Ara Parseghian was a shrewd judge of talent and he knew the big kid from East Canton would be a star. So did other coaches and scouts. Murray Warmath, coach at the University of Minnesota, said, "Page was the best high school football player I've ever seen."

At Notre Dame, Alan was an instant success. He was the star of the freshman team. Then he became the starting defensive end on the 1964 Irish squad that finished the year with a 9–1 mark. The next year a badly dislocated shoulder curtailed his play, but as a senior in 1966, he was a consensus All-America. All the pro teams wanted Page.

The Minnesota Vikings were especially interested in Alan. The Vikings were beginning to build a championship team. They already had fine defensive linemen in Carl Eller, Gary Larsen and Jim Marshall. With Page, they thought their front four would be the best in the business.

But Minnesota needed players at other positions, too. They needed their two first-round draft choices to pick up a receiver and a running back, yet they knew they would have to pick Page in the first round or lose him. In order to get Alan, they traded Tommy Mason and Hal Bedsole, both established stars, for another first-round pick. Then they drafted receiver Gene Washington, running back Clint Jones and Page, all in the first round.

When Alan came to the Vikings he weighed 270 pounds, and it was obvious that his powerful frame could carry even more weight. The Vikings considered him for both defensive end and tackle, although he preferred end, his position in college.

But the Vikings finally stationed him at tackle, and he was soon thriving at the new spot.

After three games of the 1967 season, Alan suddenly got the word from coach Grant that he might be starting game four. "It came right out of the blue," Alan said. "I hadn't been playing well, but I know I was aggressive and active on the line. I guess they liked that."

Once in the starting line-up, Page quickly made it known that he wasn't about to sit on the bench again. A few weeks later against Detroit, he was credited with six tackles, five assists and causing four fumbles. He pounced on one of the fumbles at the Viking 6-yard line to end a drive that would have won the game for Detroit. Instead the contest ended in a 10–10 tie. Most experts agreed that the man who prevented a Viking loss was Alan Page. He was named NFL Defensive Player of the Week for the first time.

The Vikings won only three games that year and finished last in the Central Division. But Alan was named Viking Rookie of the Year as well as NFL Defensive Rookie of the Year. It was already obvious that he was going to be a star.

Alan ended his rookie year weighing about 280 pounds. He was a giant, strong and agile. But the

Page (88) piles up Cleveland's Leroy Kelly in a 1967 game.

Viking coaches thought he could still improve. They wanted him to be quicker, yet if he continued to gain weight, he would only slow down.

"I resolved to lose weight," he said. "With my wife watching my diet and a lot of summer workouts, I reported at 255 in 1968. I found I hadn't lost any strength, and I was a lot quicker. I liked that. I lost another ten pounds during the season and have stayed around the 245 mark ever since. It works."

Before the 1968 season was half over, it was obvious that the Vikings were the most improved team in the league. Their big front four, known as "The Purple People Eaters," were quickly becoming the best in the business.

After a midseason 27–14 victory over the Washington Redskins, Viking defensive line coach Bob Hollway was asked to evaluate each member of his front four. He praised Carl Eller for his consistency, Gary Larsen for his strength and Jim Marshall for his great outside pass rush. Then he came to Page.

"Now, Alan Page may be the baby of the group," he said, "but you'd never know it from the way he plays. He's quick, active and relentless. He never knows when to quit. Without a doubt he's already one of the best tackles in the league."

The Vikings finished with eight wins that year, earning their first divisional title. Then in 1969 they had a sensational 12–2 record. In the playoffs they beat Los Angeles and Cleveland to win the NFL title and go on to the Super Bowl. That's where they met their match, losing 23–7 in an upset, to the Kansas City Chiefs.

But the team now had a reputation as the best defensive club in the entire league, and the front four were the prime movers in that defense. They made things happen.

Alan wasn't pleased with his play during the Super Bowl year. He had an ankle sprain in the preseason that lasted almost halfway through the schedule. He was playing full strength at the end, but the loss to the Chiefs put a damper on the whole season. When he returned in 1970, he still had the drive to be even better.

And he was, blasting through to create havoc in opposing backfields, causing fumbles, batting away passes. Against the Bears he caused a fumble, picked it up and rambled 65 yards for a touchdown.

"He has remarkable reaction at the snap," said Bud Grant. "He gets into the blocker before the man can set up properly. He's having just a great season. There's no phase of the game at which he doesn't excel."

Although Page was strong, he was most famous for his moves. "The Vikings have six basic moves to get the passer," he said. "One is to fake to the outside, smack the blocker on his helmet and go hard to the inside. That's called the slap move. Another technique is to shove both hands toward the

23

blocker's face and keep the pressure on. If the head goes back, the body will follow.

"One thing is important. You can't do it all on strength. I didn't do it on strength in college, and I'm not doing it here. As a matter of fact, the contact in pro ball hasn't been what I expected. There's actually more finesse here than in college."

At the end of 1970 the Vikings were 12–2 for the second straight season. A look at Page's statistics showed him to be a true gamebreaker, contributing immensely to many Minnesota victories throughout the year. He made seven of the team's twelve fumble recoveries, many of them in key situations. He had a big hand in victories over Chicago, Dallas and Los Angeles. Then in the playoff against San Francisco, the Minnesota defense sparkled, but the offense lacked punch. The 49ers won 17–14.

It was the same story during Alan's remarkable 1971 season. The Vikings made the playoffs for the fourth straight year but lost to Dallas for the NFC championship. That one really crushed the All-Pro tackle.

"Being the MVP hardly matters any more after that loss. We all wanted it very badly this year," he said. "After Dallas beat us, I couldn't even watch the other playoff games on television. It was like watching my own funeral."

Alan's intensity didn't always show up off the field. His wife, Lorraine, said, "Alan is two dif-

24

Alan takes a rest on the sidelines.

ferent people. On the field he's aggressive and in control of the situation. Off the field he's not always that way. He sometimes loses control. But he's beginning to overcome it. He used to be a very private person. He found it hard to be warm and friendly to outsiders. Now he's opening up and he's much friendlier with people."

Alan and Lorraine had two children of their own and adopted a third, Lorraine's teenage cousin. The responsibility of three children led

25

Alan to make plans for the time when his playing days would be over. He started a vending machine company and was involved in other business ventures.

Still going strong in 1972, Page tries to tackle the ball from Pittsburgh's Franco Harris.

Among Alan's other interests was drag racing. In late 1971 he bought a purple Dodge Charger, which he entered in a race at a strip in Coon Rapids, Minnesota. He won on his first try and broke a national record for his class.

"It's unlike anything in football," he said. "I enjoy it as a hobby, and it's not really dangerous. I sure wouldn't do anything to jeopardize my football career."

There have been a few disappointments for Page along with his successes. After his MVP year of 1971, Alan had hardly any calls to endorse products or make television commercials or personal appearances. Many superstars earn almost as much from these activities as they get from playing ball. "Alan is a very good speaker," said one of his agents. "He's a college graduate and well versed on many subjects other than football."

"I can't help but think that part of the reason is that I'm black," Page said. His complaint received wide publicity, but Page still received few invitations.

The 1972 season wasn't easy for the Vikings. Nagging injuries bothered both Page and Carl Eller, and age was creeping up on Jim Marshall and Gary Larsen. Suddenly, the Minnesota front line wasn't the solid wall of granite it had been in the past. Even with veteran quarterback Fran Tarkenton, the Viking offense was sputtering too.

So winning a Super Bowl seemed a distant goal.

But Page remained one of the great tackles in the game—rushing, driving, pursuing, tackling, doing it all.

As Bud Grant once said, "There are some people with something extra. They have the facility for turning a game around, even on one play. And if they don't—if the one play never comes—the threat of it is still there, and you have to respect them for that threat.

"These kind of people come around most infrequently. But Alan Page is without a doubt one of them."

And that is the perfect definition of a game-breaker.

2

George Blanda

At one position or another, George Blanda was a gamebreaker for nearly a quarter of a century. The grand old man of the gridiron began playing professional football in 1949, and in 1972 he was still the regular place-kicker and back-up quarterback of his team—the Oakland Raiders. As the 1973 season approached, Blanda was celebrating his 46th birthday and looking forward to another active season as a living legend.

Men who came into the game ten years after Blanda retired years ago. He was nine years older than his coach in Oakland—and eleven years older than the second oldest Raider. Some of his teammates were not even born when George broke in as a quarterback for the Chicago Bears.

29

Veteran gamebreaker George Blanda.

During his great 1971 season with Oakland, a sign appeared in the stands at the Oakland Coliseum: *God is in uniform. His number is 16.*

Blanda himself, a craggy-faced, outspoken man, had nothing but disdain for those who thought he was more than human. "One of pro football's unreasoning prejudices says a man is no longer capable of playing when he reaches 30 or 35," said George. "In many cases that's baloney. Sure, there are some factors, like injuries, that could stop a man, but desire to play and love of the game can keep you going. "Otto Graham, the finest quarterback I've ever seen, retired at 35. Don't you think he could have played another five or six years? He's 50 now, and he still handles himself better than many of these young studs right out of college.

"And I remember when I played for Sammy Baugh. He must have been at least 50 then, too. Well, Sammy should have been playing instead of coaching. He still threw as well as any quarterback on the team and punted as well as our punter. The man was amazing."

Another strange fact about Blanda is that it took him more than 20 years to become a well-known player. He held more than 40 NFL records, and yet he only reached real stardom in 1970, 22 years after his rookie season. His claim to fame was that he was football's greatest gamebreaker.

When George went to the Oakland Raiders in 1967, he was really beginning his third career in pro football. He was signed to be kicker and back-up quarterback to young Daryle Lamonica, an outstanding passer on a strong team. George would never even get in at quarterback unless Lamonica was hurt.

In three seasons, Blanda threw exactly 100 passes. Yet he completed 51 of them. Eleven went for touchdowns, and several won ballgames. In each of those three years he also scored more than 100 points as a kicker, winning several more games with his foot. No one doubted that he was a handy guy to have around.

During those three years the Raiders were one of football's better teams. In 1967 they had won the AFL championship and faced the mighty Green Bay Packers in the second Super Bowl. In 1968 and '69, they lost close pennant races to the New York Jets and Kansas City. George Blanda deserved some of the credit for the Raiders' success, but he received little attention outside of Oakland.

Then came 1970. Oakland started the season by losing two of its first three games and tying the other one. They were already in trouble—if they expected to catch the tough Kansas City Chiefs, they'd have to start moving, and fast.

With Lamonica at the controls, Oakland topped Denver and Washington to even its record at 2–2–1. Then the Raiders met the Pittsburgh Steelers. It was a make or break game, and George later admitted, "I was dying to get in, but I didn't think I had much of a chance." The old competitor was itching to play. Just kicking didn't give him enough satisfaction.

Midway through the first period, with the score tied 7–7, Lamonica pulled up lame and coach John Madden sent George into the game. On his first pass the cagey veteran connected with tight end Raymond Chester for a 29-yard touchdown. One pass and one score. The George Blanda miracle had begun.

On the very next Oakland series, George hit fleet Warren Wells on a long TD strike. Later he kicked a field goal and ended the day with a 19-yard touchdown toss to Chester. The old man had led his club to an easy 31–14 victory, and the Raiders were over .500 for the first time.

The next week Oakland played arch-rival Kansas City. Lamonica had returned, and Blanda was back on the sidelines. He watched the two teams struggle all afternoon. With time running out in the final period, Kansas City held a slim 17–14 lead. Oakland moved the ball to the Kansas City 41-yard line with time for one more play. Onto the field trotted place-kicker Blanda.

It was a 48-yard try against the wind. The Chiefs massed for one final charge, trying to unnerve the veteran with screams and shouts. Most of the huge crowd didn't think he had a chance. The snap and hold were perfect. George stepped into the ball and got it away, straight as an arrow. The ball cleared the crossbar by about a yard. Blanda had tied the game with no time left. It was a pressure finish, but the old man was the calmest guy in the place.

"I knew I had a good shot at it," he said later. "I missed a key kick at San Diego early in the year, but since then my kicking has been as good as it's been at any time in my career."

Now it was on to Cleveland. The Raiders were back in the race, but they had to keep winning. Lamonica got his team a quick 13–0 lead, and the game looked easy. But the Browns turned things around, taking a 17–13 advantage into the final period. Then Lamonica was tackled behind the line and injured. Oakland coach John Madden sent his miracle man into the game.

Suddenly it looked as if his luck had run out. The Browns quickly intercepted a Blanda pass and scored a field goal. It was now 20–13. With just four minutes left, the Raiders got the ball at their own 31. It was their last chance.

Once again, Blanda took to the air. He passed down the sideline to Wells for a 31-yard gain. Then he dumped one off to halfback Charley Smith for seven. He repeated to his other back, Hewritt Dixon, for six. But then a Cleveland blitz caught him off guard and downed him for a loss of ten. It looked bad.

Blanda took a deep breath. "We're not through yet," he said in the huddle, then called a pass play to tight end Chester. But the Browns were in a prevent defense, and the big receiver was covered. Just before he was hit by two linemen, George spied Fred Biletnikoff free on the right side and lobbed a first-down completion to him. With the ball on the

"Old George" goes back to pass for the Raiders.

14, George called Wells' number again.

"Be ready," he said to the receiver. "I can't risk an interception, and I'm gonna throw low and hard."

Then George calmly dropped back and hit Wells in the left corner of the end zone. The kick made it 20–20 with about a minute left. It looked as if George had given his team another tie. But Cleveland quarterback Bill Nelson threw a quick interception, and the Raiders had the ball near midfield with 34 seconds to go.

A couple of cautious passes fell incomplete. With three seconds left, the Raiders stopped the clock, and Blanda the quarterback became Blanda the kicker once more. But he would be kicking from 52 yards out. Only a super-kicker could make that one.

Again the snap. The ball soared high, deep— *and good!* Blanda had done it once more. He had broken open his third straight game, snatching victory from certain defeat.

Suddenly the entire country began following the exploits of this 43-year-old gamebreaker. The next week Denver led Oakland, 19–17, with four minutes to play. When George began warming up on the sideline, the fans went wild with anticipation.

"He can't do it again. He just can't," someone shouted.

Starting from the 20, George's first pass resulted

in a two-yard loss. Then he was wide on a second throw. It was third and 12. Blanda fired a clutch pass over the middle to Rod Sherman for 27 yards and kept the Raiders alive.

Next, George threw in the direction of Wells, who made a great diving catch for another first down and a gain of 35 yards. The ball was at the Denver 20. Now Blanda could work for field position, then kick the winning field goal.

But Blanda the Great kept throwing. One pass was incomplete. Then Oakland was offside, and Denver declined the penalty. Third down at the 20. George dropped back and threw to Biletnikoff at the goal line. Score! The Raiders had won the game, 24–19.

George had thrown six passes and completed four for 80 yards and a touchdown. A Denver record crowd of 50,959 went home in shock and disbelief. Around the country, the name Blanda was becoming a household word.

"Blanda is a danger to everyone over 40," wrote one columnist. "He's depriving them of that longtime excuse . . . age."

It was easy the next week against San Diego. Lamonica quarterbacked the Raiders to a tie, then moved the ball down into Charger territory with seconds left. From the 16, George kicked an easy field goal to give the Raiders a 20–17 win. It was the fifth straight week that Blanda had come off the bench to perform fourth-quarter heroics—the most

Blanda brings his foot back to kick the field goal that won his fifth game in a row, defeating the Chargers 20–17.

unbelievable stretch of gamebreaking the NFL had ever seen.

The streak couldn't go on forever—although it almost continued into the sixth week. In the closing seconds of a game against Detroit, Blanda threw a complete pass to the 3-yard line. If the play had not been called back for an off-sides penalty, it could have beat Detroit. But this time the Lions held on to win.

As Blanda left the field that day, veteran Detroit linebacker Wayne Walker came over and said, "Not this time, old-timer." It wasn't the loss that hurt Blanda the most, but Walker's calling him "old-timer." George didn't consider himself old.

Several weeks later, Blanda tossed a TD pass and kicked both extra points in a 14–13 win over the Jets. Thanks to George, the Raiders were in the playoffs again.

The Raiders' story didn't have a happy ending, and Blanda was on the field when the Raiders lost their chance to go to the Super Bowl. Playing the Colts for the AFC championship, the Raiders trailed 10–0 when Lamonica was injured in a collision with big Bubba Smith. Blanda came in, kicked a field goal, then tossed a TD pass to Biletnikoff to tie it up. For a while it looked as if the miracle man would do it again.

But the Colts were a team with a mission. They forged ahead again, 20–10. George threw one more scoring pass, to Wells, but Baltimore marched right back to match it. The Raiders were done, losing 27–17. And 43-year-old George Blanda sat down in front of his locker and cried. When a reporter reminded him of his fine afternoon statistically, George said, "Don't talk about it. The score's all I remember."

Old George had completed 17 passes in 32 attempts for 271 yards and two touchdowns. He did throw three interceptions, but he had been playing catch-up football against a top defensive team. Under the circumstances, it was still another remarkable performance.

Blanda was the most honored athlete in the country that year. He was named the NFL's Most Valuable Player and *Sport* magazine's Man of the Year. But he said to one reporter who wanted to interview him, "Where were you 20 years ago when I needed you the most?"

The Blanda story goes back to Youngwood, Pennsylvania, where George was born on September 17, 1927. His father was a Czech immigrant who worked in the mines to scratch out a living for his wife, seven sons and four daughters. He was a tough man who was determined that his sons would not follow him to a life in the mines.

George learned about hard work and competition at an early age. The Great Depression made jobs scarce, yet George found a variety of odd jobs while he was going through school. He was also

41

competing with his six brothers. Competition was a way of life in the coal country of Pennsylvania, and George often pointed out that many great athletes came from the region. Some of the stars who spent their boyhoods in towns near Youngwood were Stan Musial, Johnny Lujack, Arnold Palmer, John Unitas, Pistol Pete Maravich and Joe Namath.

As a high schooler in Youngwood, George was a great all-around athlete. Besides being a football and basketball star, he was a one-man track team, the sole representative of Youngwood, competing in track events, discus, shot put and javelin.

By the time he graduated, he was a star half-back and kicker. He got a scholarship to Kentucky and played under Paul "Bear" Bryant, one of the most dynamic coaches in college football. After four successful seasons as a quarterback and line-backer, George was drafted by the Chicago Bears after the 1948 season. He also had an offer from a team in the old All-America Conference, but George Halas, owner-coach of the Bears, talked him into signing for $6,000.

Thus began a decade of frustration for Blanda. He never got along with Halas and fought for years to win a starting job. When he joined the team, veterans Sid Luckman and Johnny Lujack were the top quarterbacks. George threw a touchdown pass in his first play from scrimmage, but he was still third string.

After Luckman and Lujack retired, George

shared the position with a succession of mediocre signal-callers, such as Ed Brown, Zeke Bratkowski and Rudy Bukich. Only once did George play a nearly full season. That was in 1953 when he threw 362 passes and completed 169 for 14 TD's. But the Bears won only three games that year, and the next season he was a part-timer again.

He remained the Bears' regular kicker, however, once booting 156 straight conversions without a miss, and he scored more than 500 points for them. But when he threw just 19 passes in 1957 and only seven in 1958, he knew his days with the Bears were numbered. He told Halas he wouldn't stay on as just a kicker. One word led to another, and the coach announced Blanda's retirement. A brief trial with the Colts didn't work, and Blanda was out of football during the 1959 season. He was just 32 years old.

But he wasn't forgotten. The next year the American Football League was formed, and the Houston Oilers promptly signed the veteran to be their quarterback. Finally getting the chance to play regularly, Blanda didn't waste any time loosening up the old wing. He came to throw the football, and in the next six seasons he firmly established himself as the top passer in the AFL.

He pitched the Oilers to a pair of AFL championships. In 1961 he tied Y.A. Tittle's pro record of 36 touchdown passes in a season. He also tied a record by throwing for seven touchdowns in a

Blanda throws a pass for the Houston Oilers in 1964. With Houston he set many all-time AFL passing and scoring records.

single game. He helped the 1961 Oilers become the only pro team in history to gain more than 6,000 yards and score more than 500 points. In 1961 his favorite receiver, Charley Hennigan, caught passes for 1,746 yards, a pro record; and three years later Hennigan set another mark by grabbing 101 passes in 14 games.

Besides his throwing arm, George still had the big foot. His kicking with the Oilers accounted for another 500-plus points. He also became a big booster and spokesman for the new league. Even after it merged with the NFL, he continued to praise the old AFL.

"The pass receivers on the Oilers were every bit as good as those I've thrown to before and since," he said. "They had the same quickness and ability to get open. To tell you the truth, I think the AFL was capable of beating the NFL in a Super Bowl game as far back as 1960 or 1961."

By 1966, Oiler fortunes had declined and the team was rebuilding. Blanda was 39 years old, and he was shipped out to Oakland after the season to begin career number three. He was a part-time quarterback and a full-time kicker, but he still looked forward to those opportunities to throw the football. And he rarely failed to deliver.

In 1968 he replaced Lamonica in one game against Kansas City. All he did was complete eleven of fourteen passes for 129 yards, a club record for accuracy. Playing against Denver the next week, he passed for four touchdowns, including a 94-yarder to Warren Wells. Then it was back to the bench, but only after he was named Offensive Player of the Week.

In 1969 he threw the ball just 13 times. He failed to get into the AFL championship game, even after Lamonica severely bruised his hand and couldn't grip the football properly. He complained bitterly, and prior to the 1970 season Oakland put him on waivers, making it possible for other teams to buy him cheaply.

Fortunately, no one picked him up. Then the Raiders' new place-kicker failed, and their young quarterback Ken Stabler was slow in developing, so they decided to bring Blanda back. At 43, he saved the season for his team and was named the league's MVP.

"Retire!" George Blanda exclaimed whenever a reporter brought the subject up. "Listen, football is a privilege that some men are lucky to enjoy longer than others. I haven't the slightest intention of retiring, not this year, next year, or ten years from now. Since I was five years old I've been running up and down football fields. Why should I stop now?"

Maybe sportswriter Wells Twombly said it best. Writing in the *Sporting News* about Blanda, Twombly said, "Some afternoon, decades hence, when John Brodie's grandson is throwing his first pass for the Stanford varsity, they will come down to the Oakland Raiders' bench, reluctantly tap Blanda on his shoulder pads, and lead him off to Canton, Ohio [home of the pro football Hall of Fame]. That's where the man belongs."

With quarterback Daryle Lamonica holding, Blanda boots another field goal for the Raiders.

3

Larry Little

It was late October of 1971. The Miami Dolphins were playing the New York Jets at rainy, wind-swept Shea Stadium. Like most quarterbacks, Miami's Bob Griese didn't like to pass on blustery afternoons. He kept handing the ball to his big running backs, Jim Kiick and Larry Csonka, and they proceeded to eat up chunks of yardage around the Jet flanks.

Time and again, Kiick and Csonka came around the ends, gaining six, seven, eight yards a play. They were making it look easy.

"Man, can those two guys run," moaned a Jet fan in disbelief.

"Why don't Baker and Tannen do something about it?" asked another.

Ralph Baker and Steve Tannen, the Jets' left linebacker and left cornerback, were supposed to turn a sweep toward the middle of the field and then tackle the ball-carrier. But today they weren't succeeding. Every time Kiick or Csonka galloped around the right side, a 6-foot-1, 265-pound thunderbolt sprinted out ahead of them, blasting everyone, including Baker and Tannen, right out of the play.

The thunderbolt was named Larry Little. As Miami's regular right guard, Little was making quite a name for himself. In fact many football people considered him the very best offensive lineman in the entire National Football League.

Miami won the ballgame, 30–14, as both Csonka and Kiick rushed for more than 100 yards. The two backs were surrounded by reporters in the Miami locker room after the game. But one reporter drifted over to big number 66, Larry Little, who had done perhaps more than anyone to break the running backs free and break the game open for the Dolphins.

"It makes me feel good to see those guys run like that," Little said, gesturing toward Csonka and Kiick. "I feel the same way when Bob [Griese] throws a TD pass, or Paul [Warfield] catches one. I feel that I'm part of it.

"I know guards don't get much recognition. That's all right with me. I'm just interested in knocking people down and getting some respect.

In the midst of the Miami offensive line,
Larry Little (66) gets ready to charge.

Sometimes it was Tannen today, sometimes Baker, sometimes it was somebody else in a white suit. I have tremendous pride in my ability as a blocker, and I like my job.

"When I see those number 20s and 30s coming," he said, referring to the numbers worn by defensive backfield men, "I know it's one of those little cornerbacks and I don't really mind running over those guys. I don't like simply cutting them down—I want to run right through them and keep on going. That way, the next time you come at them, they're gonna know just who it is."

Jim Kiick, one of the ball-carriers who benefits from Little's pile-driving, once said, "With Larry Little blocking for me, I don't have to run over anyone, I just run past them or around them. He goes in first and cleans them right out."

As for recognition, Larry Little has gotten plenty of it. At the end of the 1970 and 1971 seasons, he was voted the best offensive lineman in the American Conference by the NFL players, the men who should know best. In addition, he finally achieved his long-standing goal of being an All-Pro when the Professional Football Writers Association, the Associated Press, *Pro Football Weekly*, and the *Sporting News* all placed him on the 1971 and 1972 All-NFL teams.

Larry Little had come a long way in his first six years as a professional football player. At one time he was a 300-pound butterball who played only

Little has pulled from his guard position and is racing around end to provide interference for the ball-carrier. A Colt defender is too late to stop him.

part-time with the San Diego Chargers. He was even beginning to wonder if he would ever make it in the pro game. He had chosen pro football as a way out of tough times, and yet it seemed for a while that it would let him down.

The tough times started early for Larry. He was born in Groveland, Georgia, in November of 1945, the second of six children. His family moved to Miami when he was still in grade school. Both his parents worked very hard, his father as a laborer and his mother as a maid. Although the family had enough to eat, they lived in a poor black neighborhood in Miami.

"My mother was great," Larry recalled. "She always provided for us, but not for herself. Sometimes she'd go for years without buying a dress. So I guess you'd say we were poor, but we were never hungry. I ate the best of anyone. My mother was a great cook, and when the rest of the family had something I didn't like, she'd cook something else separately, just for me."

In grade school Larry got into some minor trouble. One time, Larry and some of his friends were suspended from school for five days. The principal sent Larry home with a note about the suspension, but he didn't give it to his parents.

"The next day he got up and dressed, just like he was going to school," said Mrs. Little. "But a friend of mine saw him on the street during the day, and I knew something was up. When he finally owned up, he got the worst punishment of his life—with a strap. Then we took him over to the school and made him apologize to his teacher. He never did that kind of thing again."

Larry grew up within walking distance of the Orange Bowl, the stadium in which the Dolphins now play. On Saturdays he and his friends watched the crowds arriving at the big bowl to see college games, and heard the cheering when the home team scored. (The Dolphins had not yet been organized, and Miami had no pro football team.)

"Hearing those crowds always made us want to play," Larry said. "Sometimes we'd walk to the nearest park, or we'd just play on the streets. And we played tackle then, with four or five guys on a side and no equipment. Needless to say, we picked up some pretty good bumps and bruises.

"I always wanted to play fullback in those days. Since I was bigger than most of the guys, I guess I thought I could run right over them. But I had my fill of that, especially when the Chargers tried me at fullback during my rookie season. I soon learned that I'd rather hit than be hit. When you run with the ball or go out for passes, guys are always hitting you around your knees. You can keep that kind of stuff. I don't need it."

Larry's older brother, George, was the person most responsible for urging him to pursue football. At Booker T. Washington High in Miami, Larry was a good 210-pound lineman. But George urged him to work even harder—at football and at his studies. Larry's work paid off when he earned a scholarship to Bethune-Cookman College, also in Miami.

"I can be honest about it," Larry said later. "I was exposed to everything when I was growing up, and I'd be lying if I tried to say I never did anything wrong. I was lucky that George kept pushing me."

By the time Larry was a sophomore at Bethune-Cookman, he weighed 240 pounds and was still growing. He played tackle on both offense and defense in his first two varsity seasons, then concentrated on defense as a senior. By that time Larry tipped the scales at around 260 pounds, and he was looking forward to pro football. Remembering his family's poverty, he saw football as a way out.

Then came disappointment. Although he had been captain of the Bethune-Cookman team during his final season and had made the Ebony Press All-America team, no pro team drafted him.

"It was a real blow to me," he said, "a big disappointment."

Suddenly in the days after the draft, the pro teams got interested in Larry, and many of them made him offers. He couldn't understand why they had changed their minds so quickly.

He finally signed with San Diego. That summer he reported to his first professional training camp. First there was talk of making him a fullback.

LARRY LITTLE

Larry could run 40 yards in 4.9 seconds—a fast time for such a big man—and the San Diego coaches could imagine his 273 pounds crashing through enemy lines. But Larry wasn't fast enough. He was moved back to defensive tackle. Then Charger coach Sid Gillman worried that Larry was too short at 6-foot-1 for the defensive line, and decided to move him to guard on offense.

While he was being shifted from position to position, Larry took out his frustrations at the training table. The food was good and plentiful, and by the time the season started, Larry weighed nearly 300 pounds. His weight gain had been phenomenal. Teammates watched him devour the goodies, especially his favorite, fried chicken, and began calling him "Chicken Little."

Coach Gillman didn't find it humorous. In fact, when someone mentioned Larry's weight, Gillman would roar, "I can't seem to motivate the man. And I can't stand a person I can't motivate."

Gillman felt his ulcers rumbling every time he saw his rookie guard take another big mouthful. But he kept Larry's tremendous potential in mind and kept him as a reserve through 1967 and 1968.

Larry played regularly only on the Charger special teams and continued to show promise there. "Larry does an exceptional job blocking on kickoff returns," said offensive line coach Joe Madro. "He's got all the physical tools—big, strong, tough,

fast, mobile. I know he's a good pulling guard and running blocker. If he can put it together and drop a few pounds, he's got a shot at starting."

The starting job never came. Deciding that Larry was forever destined to be a bloated blocker, Coach Gillman finally traded him. In the summer of 1969 he shipped Larry to Miami in exchange for a defensive back named Mack Lamb, who had been a high school teammate of Larry's.

"I'm bitter," Larry said when asked about the trade. "I really don't see the reason for it. I was starting to play more in San Diego and just beginning to fit in." Still, Miami was his hometown—things could have been worse.

When Larry arrived in Miami the Dolphins were preparing for their fourth season. The season before, they had achieved their best record, finishing with five wins in fourteen games. Coach George Wilson had been seeking more protection for his promising young quarterback, Bob Griese. The coach expected Larry to bolster the offensive line.

Like Sid Gillman in San Diego, the easygoing Wilson worried about Larry's weight. He urged his new guard to diet, and Larry tried, working his weight down to 285. When the season started, Larry alternated at right guard with veteran Billy Neighbors, who expected to retire at the end of the year. Coach Wilson figured that by alternating, the

Adjusting his arm pads, Little follows the action while the defensive team is on the field.

59

vet could help the youngster and there wouldn't be
too much pressure on Larry.

An early-season knee injury slowed Larry's
progress, but by midseason he was seeing more action and fans were beginning to notice a new dimension in the Dolphin attack. For the first time in
their short history, Miami was running to the outside. Young backs Larry Csonka and Jim Kiick
were beginning to circle the ends and gain yardage.
And one big reason was the aggressive play of
Larry Little.

His ferocity on sweeps impressed George Wilson. "He makes me awfully glad I'm not playing
any more," Wilson admitted. "I feel sorry for guys
who have to take the kind of blocks Larry throws
around."

Despite Larry's flashes of brilliance, it was still
a season of learning. He found that every game was
different as he faced many different defensive linemen. "You've got to try something different each
week," he said. "No two defensive linemen do the
same things, so you've got to learn to adjust, and
quickly."

Sadly, the Dolphins weren't keeping pace with
their new young lineman. The team had seemed to
be on the rise, improving its record each year. But
1969 turned into a disaster. By season's end the
club dropped back into the AFL cellar with a 3–
10–1 mark. Changes had to be made. Coach Wilson was the first to go.

Most of the Dolphin players liked the easygoing Wilson. When the team's management announced that the new coach would be Don Shula, the highly successful coach of the Baltimore Colts, the players were worried. Shula had a reputation as a hard-driving taskmaster. Would he make drastic changes and major trades to form his kind of team? The mood of the Dolphins changed after Shula arrived, but there was no radical housecleaning.

Shula had a simple philosophy, and he expected every member of his team to adhere to it. "You set a goal to be the best and then work hard every hour, every day, striving to reach that goal," he said. "If you allow yourself to settle for anything less than number one, you're cheating yourself."

Shula particularly wanted Larry Little to apply this philosophy. The coach had seen Little in action and recognized his tremendous, explosive potential. Larry was on the way to realizing that potential, but Shula saw the need for additional improvement.

"I told Larry he could be one of the very best guards in all of football," the coach said. "But I felt he was still playing heavy at 285. I suggested he lose another 20 pounds. It wasn't easy for him, pushing away from that table. But he worked, and he did it."

The hard work was already showing results—of the wrong kind—in August of 1970. Larry had been pushing himself, losing weight, and working hard to improve his already devastating blocking skills. During a rough practice session he was standing near defensive line coach Monte Clark when he suddenly collapsed from exhaustion.

"One minute he was there, the next he was gone," Clark said.

Larry recovered quickly, and when the 1970 season got underway, he weighed just 264 pounds. He was lean and mean and raring to go.

The four men happiest to see the new Larry Little were running backs Csonka, Kiick and Mercury Morris, and Dolphin quarterback Griese. On the famous Dolphin sweeps, Larry was quicker than ever, pulling out of his guard position and turning the corner ahead of his backs. Often he cleared a path wide enough for Humpty Dumpty to walk through. On pass plays, he helped form a blocking wall around Griese that even the best pass rushers had a hard time penetrating.

Helped by some shrewd trades and by their new training and spirit, the Dolphins began winning. After splitting its first eight games, the team came on to take its last six in a row, including an impressive 34–17 victory over the Baltimore Colts. The Dolphins' 10–4 record gave them second place in the AFC East Division. And they qualified for the playoffs by having the best record of any second-place team in the Conference.

During the season Csonka gained 874 yards, Kiick 658, and Morris 409. And the runners gave

In the 1972 AFC championship game, Little (66) bowls over Pittsburgh's Mean Joe Greene.

credit to their big blocker. "Running behind Larry Little is like running behind a truck," said Kiick. The players of the AFC agreed, naming Larry the top offensive lineman in the Conference.

Larry was pleased, but not satisfied. "I want to win the championship and I want to be All-Pro," he said.

The championship didn't come. Miami lost to Oakland, 21–14, in the first round of the playoffs, and everyone went home, vowing to come back in '71.

Between seasons, Larry Little was becoming a very busy man. He was active in civic affairs around Miami. He and several other Dolphins opened the Gold Coast Camp for underprivileged youngsters. Rudy Barber, a former Dolphin lineman, explained the camp this way. "There are so many wrong things going on where these boys are growing up. Many are around dope pushers, dropouts . . . and they'll be like what they see. We just want to steer them in the right direction."

Larry's commitment to the camp ran deep. "Most of these kids want to play pro football," he said. "Every kid dreams about it. But I tell them to get their high school education first. Then, if they have the opportunity to continue on to college, I urge them to go.

"I was lucky. I made it into pro ball. But I've seen so many guys who wanted to play forced into another line of work. And man, they really find themselves out in the cold without that degree.

"A lot of these kids think if they can play football, they don't have to know anything else. Not true. I always tell them that they might get in the door because they're athletes, but to stay there they have to produce. And if they don't know anything, they won't be able to do the job."

Larry knew what it was like on the other side of the fence. He gave freely of his time and energy to help the youngsters, and his efforts earned him the Citizen of the Year Award from a Miami fraternal organization and an honorary degree from a Florida college.

On the football field Larry remained as aggressive as ever. Coach Shula had his 1971 Dolphins primed and ready to go. Running the power sweep with more effectiveness than ever, Dolphin runners racked up yardage and opponents. Csonka went over the 1,000-yard mark, and Kiick wasn't far behind. As usual, the man in front of both of them was often Larry Little.

"I've had some good games and some not-so-good games," said Larry near the season's end. "Just when you think you're satisfied with a performance, you watch the films of it and find you made some stupid mistakes. It never fails."

After playing to a tie with Denver in the opener, and losing to the Jets in game number three, Shula's Miamians reeled off eight wins in a row. Two late-season losses brought their final mark to 10–3–1, but they won their first divisional title and went into the playoffs for the second year in a row.

Before the playoffs, Larry said, "We know what it's like to win now, and believe me, it's the only way to enjoy the game. What happened at Oakland last year . . . well, we don't want it to happen again."

The Dolphins started the playoffs by defeating the Kansas City Chiefs, 27–24, in the longest foot-

65

ball game ever. It went almost two overtime periods before Garo Yepremian's 37-yard field goal settled the issue. Then a week later the team played perfect football, trouncing arch-rival Baltimore, 21–0. Now only the Super Bowl remained.

Before the big game, Larry was asked what he planned to do against the Dallas Cowboys, especially defensive tackle Jethro Pugh.

"I've just seen Pugh on films," he told reporters. "He looks strong and active, and he has about the longest arms I've ever seen. He's also five inches taller than I am. So I'll have to keep his hands off me and keep him directly in front of me. It won't be easy."

It wasn't easy for any of the Dolphins. For one of the few times all year, the Miami offense couldn't move the ball. There were two rare fumbles, both on inside running plays, and Griese couldn't pass against the tough Dallas defense. Although Larry played Pugh to a stand-off, the Cowboys prevailed, 24–3, and stopped the Dolphins from becoming champions in just their sixth year of existence. They were still the first team to get that far in such a short time.

As for Larry, the postseason honors continued to roll in. He was the top AFC offensive lineman again and fulfilled his dream of making the All-Pro team. The only thing he had been denied was the joy of winning the big one.

All that ended in 1972, and it ended in a way

the football world will not soon forget. The Dolphins started winning and kept winning. Quarterback Griese was hurt in the fifth game, but veteran Earl Morrall stepped in and led the team without a backward step.

When the regular season ended, the Miamians were undefeated, setting an NFL record of 14 straight victories in one season. Along the way,

Little (66) leads the interference for ball-carrier Mercury Morris (22) in the 1973 Super Bowl.

Dolphin runners set a new standard for yards gained. Both Csonka and Mercury Morris went over the 1,000 yard mark, and Kiick was not far behind. And a big reason for the runners' great season was Larry Little.

In the postseason playoffs the Dolphins first toppled the Cleveland Browns. Then they met the Pittsburgh Steelers for the AFC title, and Larry battled Pittsburgh's great tackle, Mean Joe Greene, coming out on top as Miami won 21–17.

Finally, to cap off a perfect season, Miami defeated the tough Washington Redskins, 14–7, in the Super Bowl. The Dolphins were world champions.

The team, put together for the first time in 1966, had reached the top in its seventh season. It was an impressive football machine with many important parts. And most experts agree that the Miami steamroller wouldn't be quite the same team without its gamebreaking right guard, Larry Little.

4

Jim Plunkett

When you have turned in the greatest performances in memory as a college quarterback, what do
you do for an encore? That was the question facing
Jim Plunkett when he joined the cellar-dwelling
New England Patriots in 1971. He had won the
Heisman Trophy as best college player in 1970 and
had set several NCAA records in his three seasons
at Stanford University. Football fans all over the
country admired him and would be watching his
every move with the Patriots. Yet big-name quarterbacks had failed before, and with better teams
than the Patriots.

According to Plunkett, the first step was to take
command. "Quarterbacks have to carry a degree of
authority," he said during his rookie season.

"They've got to earn the full respect of the team, and that's what I've always strived for. When I step into a huddle, I call the play with as much confidence as I can. I feel it's going to work, and I want all the other guys to feel the same way, too."

Respect must come gradually for a rookie quarterback, however. He is calling plays and giving orders to men much older and more experienced than he. Jim worked slowly to gain the Pats' confidence. Then during a midseason game with the Buffalo Bills he played the kind of game that commanded the respect of the whole team.

Jim Plunkett calls signals for the New England Patriots.

On the very first series of downs, Jim was dropped by two Buffalo pass rushers. As he started to get up he felt a sharp pain in the back of his left leg. It was a hamstring pull, and he knew that in the cold, damp New England weather, it wasn't going to get any better.

The Bills sensed they had the rookie signal caller on the ropes. Now they pursued him with fire in their eyes. With the injury, Jim couldn't always move fast enough to get away from them, but he stayed in the game and played spectacularly. He brought the Pats from behind twice and eventually led the team to a 28–20 win. He completed nine of sixteen passes for 218 yards and four touchdowns.

"Jim showed us he could play hurt," said Jon Morris, the Pats' center and one of the team leaders. "He didn't complain once about the leg. We knew how badly it hurt, but he tossed those TD passes like he was at a Sunday picnic. You've really got to admire him for the way he performed."

One Patriot wasn't surprised. He was rookie receiver Randy Vataha, who had played with Jim at Stanford. "I knew the leg injury wouldn't stop Jim," said Vataha. "He loves the game too much for that. He'd have to be dragged off the field bodily before he'd call it quits. People just don't realize how strong he is. And on the TD pass I caught, he waited until that last second, even though he knew he'd get creamed again. Jim's always had guts."

Jim needed a special kind of courage from the

time he was a youngster in San Jose, California. He was born in December of 1947. As a Mexican-American, he had things a little harder than others in San Jose. To make things more difficult, both his parents were blind.

Although the Plunketts were never desperately poor, Jim and his two sisters took odd jobs after school and during vacations to help out. Jim worked at a grocery store, sold papers and pumped gas. When he was old enough, he did construction work.

By the time he reached the eighth grade he was already 5-foot-11 and weighed 150 pounds. One day that year he found out he could throw a football. "It happened just like that," he said. "I picked up the ball and discovered I could wing it further than anyone else my age."

When Jim entered his junior year at James Lick High in San Jose, he was 6-foot-3 and weighed more than 200 pounds. As quarterback, he led his team to 17 wins in 18 games. He received many offers of football scholarships. Wanting to be close to his parents, he chose nearby Stanford University, a top academic school which also had a big league football program.

At Stanford, Jim's career almost ended before it began. Just before the freshman football season began, a routine medical check revealed a thyroid tumor in the left side of his neck. He needed an operation. Fortunately, the tumor was not cancerous, but Jim admitted that the tumor scared him more than any football game ever did.

Nevertheless, the damage was done. Jim didn't play until the final three games of the year. In spring practice with the varsity, Jim played poorly and became a third-string quarterback who didn't even suit up for the games. Late in the season he still had not gotten into a game, and coach John Ralston decided to red-shirt him. This meant that Jim wouldn't appear in any of the remaining games, and he would still be eligible for three years of varsity play.

Early in the 1968 season Plunkett became Stanford's first-string quarterback. In his first start, against San Jose State, he completed ten passes in thirteen tries for 277 yards and four touchdowns. Stanford routed San Jose, 68–20. One of the greatest collegiate careers in history had begun.

Jim had already set some records in his sophomore year. He gained 2,156 yards passing, more than any player in the history of the Pacific Eight Conference. Stanford, which was accustomed to losing teams, won six, lost three and tied one.

Jim continued his record-setting pace the next year, leading Stanford to a 7–2–1 record. Both losses were heartbreakers: a 36–35 defeat by Purdue, and a 26–24 loss to Southern Cal. Jim set an-

Plunkett's special kind of courage brought him instant stardom in the NFL.

other host of records, completing 197 passes (nearly 20 per game) for 2,673 yards, improving his own Pacific Eight record.

Now Jim had to make a decision. He had a year of eligibility left at Stanford, but he was also eligible for the pro draft. If he turned pro, it was obvious that he could sign for a bundle of money. Yet Jim decided to stay at Stanford another year.

"It wasn't really a difficult decision for me," he said. "I wanted to finish what I started. We had a shot at the Pacific Eight title and the Rose Bowl. All my coaches and teammates were building toward this for three years. If I turned pro, I'd be letting them down. We all wanted to reach the same goal together. We're always telling kids not to drop out, to finish school and work toward goals. I wouldn't be setting much of an example if I quit to play pro ball."

The decision took more courage than Jim admitted. If he were injured during his senior season, he might never be able to earn big money in professional ball. Even if he had a poor season, his market value would drop. But Jim wasn't planning to have a bad season.

In the opener against Arkansas he completed 22 of 39 passes for 262 yards and led Stanford to a 34–28 victory. They were off and running. After an upset loss to Purdue, Jim came back to complete a sensational 19 of 31 for 275 yards in a 24–14 win over arch-rival Southern Cal. This victory helped

Stanford gain its first conference title and its first Rose Bowl invitation since 1952. Two late-season losses left the team with an 8–3 record. Now they faced unbeaten and top-ranked Ohio State in the Rose Bowl. With a record crowd of 103,838 fans jamming the huge stadium at Pasadena, Jim went to work. On the second play of the game, he dropped back and tossed a touchdown pass to end Bobby Moore. It looked like a great start, but then the play was called back for a penalty.

Jim wasn't dismayed, though. "We knew we had to hit them in a hurry. The penalty could have demoralized us. I knew we had to do it again. The guys knew it, too."

This time the club marched steadily downfield. Jim kept the Buckeyes off balance by calling running plays, and his halfback finally scored on a short plunge. The kick made it 7–0. Next time Stanford got the ball, Jim threw what looked like another scoring pass. But end Randy Vataha dropped the ball in the end zone. Stanford had to settle for a field goal, and the score was 10–0.

Then favored Ohio State took over. Buckeye quarterback Rex Kern dazzled the Indians with his ball-handling, and running backs John Brockington and Leo Hayden ate up yardage. Now the Buckeyes were marching downfield for a score. Minutes later, they scored again. At half time it was a 14–10 game, with Ohio State in front.

No one scored in the third period. Then Jim

started throwing again. He threw to Moore and Vataha on sideline patterns and to his backs over the
middle. Finally he passed to Moore on the 2. On
the next play the fullback plowed over for the
touchdown. Stanford led 17–14, threatening a
major upset.

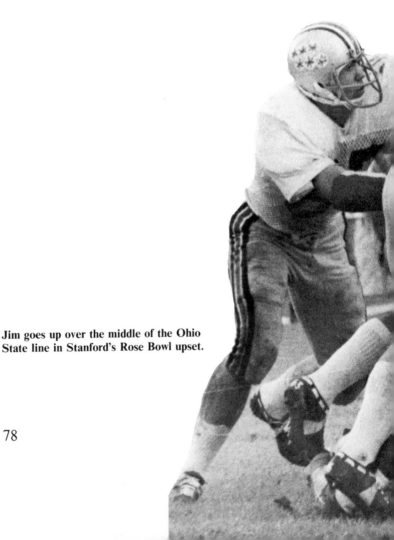

Jim goes up over the middle of the Ohio
State line in Stanford's Rose Bowl upset.

78

When Kern tried to match Jim's passing magic, Stanford intercepted the ball. Coolly, Jim moved his club downfield again. This time he spotted Vataha cutting into the end zone and threw a perfect pass. The speedy end held on this time, and Stanford had a 24–14 lead. A pair of late field goals by each team made the final score 27–17, and Stanford had upset the top team in the country. Once again Jim was the dominant player, hitting on 20 of 30 passes for 265 yards.

Looking back, Jim's college career had been almost unbelievable. He set the NCAA mark for yards gained passing (7,544) and total yards gained (7,887). In his last year he won the Heisman and Maxwell awards and was named to nearly every All-America team. To pro teams, he was the best quarterback prospect to come along in years. Not only was he a record-setter, but he was big and had proved to be durable.

Jim knew that the New England Patriots had first choice in the upcoming draft. But the team had veteran quarterback Joe Kapp, and people doubted the Pats could afford two high-priced quarterbacks. Would they trade away their draft rights to the young star?

The Pats picked Plunkett. Then before Jim reported to training camp, Kapp walked out in a contract dispute. That left Jim and holdover Mike Taliaferro to compete for the starting job.

In the exhibition games Taliaferro called the

signals, with Jim relieving for short periods of time. Yet Jim performed as well as Taliaferro when he got the chance. Coach John Mazur and general manager Upton Bell finally decided to go with Plunkett. He was a big, strong rookie and could only improve. Taliaferro had been around for eight years and had reached his peak. When the regular season opened Jim Plunkett was the Pats' starting quarterback and the pressure was on.

Reporters asked Jim about the pressure. They reminded him that the top rookie quarterback in 1970, Terry Bradshaw of the Steelers, had had a miserable season.

"It's easy to become frustrated like Terry did," Jim said. "You do things in college that you think you can do here, and when they don't work, you wonder what's wrong. I know there'll be setbacks, but there will also be progress. If the frustration doesn't linger too long, I should be all right."

The Pats faced the powerful Oakland Raiders in the first game of the season. Jim called running plays and threw short sideline passes in the first half. He didn't move his team too well, but neither did the Raiders. At the half, Oakland led 6–0.

At half time, coach Mazur decided to change strategy. "Let's open it up—we might surprise them," he told his club.

Jim began throwing, sticking mostly to short passes. He drove the Pats downfield, slowly but steadily, and fullback Jim Nance took the ball over on a plunge from the 2. The kick was good, and New England led 7–6.

Next time they got the ball, the Pats moved again. With a third-down play at his own 34, Jim faded to pass. He spied his old Stanford teammate, Vataha, racing the Oakland defenders far downfield. He pumped once and threw. Vataha grabbed the perfect pass and carried it all the way to the 27. The Patriot fans went wild. Three plays later, Jim tossed a swing pass to tight end Roland Moss. Moss grabbed the ball at the 10 and waltzed into the end zone untouched. It was Jim's first touchdown pass in the NFL, and it gave the team a 14–6 lead.

The Patriots scored twice more on field goals, and New England had upset the Raiders, 20–6. Plunkett and the surprising Patriot defense had done it. Jim completed just six of fifteen passes in his pro debut, but he looked good when it counted.

The following week things were different. New England was trounced 34–7 by Detroit. The only bright spot was a 61-yard TD bomb from Jim to Randy Vataha. Jim was disappointed, but he didn't expect to win them all.

"I wasn't sharp out there today," he said, "and I know it. But you've got to forget about a game like this once it's over. You can learn from it, but you can't let it get to you. There's a certain type of mentality associated with a loser. You never have any real confidence. And we can't let that happen here. We've got to keep thinking we're going to win. And if we play well, we will win."

As the season went on it became obvious that the Pats weren't going to work any miracles. They would lose more than they won. But Jim was learning and impressing people. Bubba Smith, Baltimore's All-Pro lineman, called him "unbelievable," even though the Colts drubbed the Patriots 23–3.

Losses to Miami, Dallas and San Francisco and a win against Buffalo gave the Pats a 2–5 record at midseason. San Francisco quarterback John Brodie commented, "Jim Plunkett is going to be great. But he's got to take command of the Patriot offense, put his own personality into it before it will click." Brodie also thought that Jim should be throwing the ball more.

The rookie took the advice, firing a barrage of TD passes in a win over Houston. Then in Buffalo he was injured but still came back to win. Bills coach Harvey Johnson marveled at Jim's improvement. "He's really learned to control himself in that pocket," Johnson said. "He waits until his receiver gets free, then lets fly. And he doesn't worry about getting hit."

The Patriots had to struggle at times during the year. But two late-season games showed the great potential of their young quarterback. Against the powerful Miami Dolphins, Jim came on the field trailing 7–0 in the first quarter. In all the previous games, he had opened with running plays. Facing

Plunkett throws over the outstretched arms of an Atlanta defender early in the 1972 season.

the Dolphins, he came out winging.

He threw the ball the first seven times he got his hands on it, completing each pass and driving the Pats downfield. When he finally called a running play, Nance went over for the touchdown. Then the Pats recovered a Miami fumble on the kickoff. With the ball at the 26, Jim dropped back and threw a strike to Vataha. Touchdown! He had his team ahead, 14–7.

Charlie Gogolak kicked two Patriot field goals and Yepremian kicked one for the Dolphins, making the score 20–10 at the half. Then in the third quarter, Jim hit Vataha for a 51-yard gain and came right back to hit him with a 25-yard TD toss, putting the game out of the Dolphins' reach. New England won 34–13.

In the final game of the season, against the Colts in Baltimore, New England was looking for its first win away from home. The Pats wanted this one badly.

Jim threw one touchdown pass and led another long drive for a score. At the same time, the New England defense held. With two minutes left, the Pats led 14–10. But the Patriots were in a hole. The ball was on their own 12-yard line, and it was third down. If Jim couldn't get the first down, the Pats would have to punt, and the Colts' master, John Unitas, would have a good chance to drive for the winning touchdown.

In the huddle Jim made a surprising decision.

Instead of playing it safe and running a draw play or sweep, he looked at receiver Randy Vataha and said one word: "Go!"

Plunkett was risking a long pass play. He took the snap, faked a running play, then dropped back. Vataha was outracing two Colt defenders, and Jim threw the ball as far as he could. Vataha grabbed the pigskin a step ahead of his pursuers and raced away to the end zone. It was an 88-yard pass play and locked the game up, 21–10. Plunkett had broken open another one.

By season's end Jim was an acknowledged star. He had beat back the pressure to become a genuine gamebreaker in his rookie year. In fact, he even became the first NFL quarterback ever to call every single offensive play for his team during the full slate of 14 games.

In completing 158 of 328 passes for 2,158 yards and 19 TD's, Jim led his team from its dismal 2–12 record of 1970 to instant respectability with a 6–8 mark. His 19 TD tosses represented the second highest total ever by a rookie, more than Fran Tarkenton or Joe Namath, who each had 18 in his rookie season. Jim was named the AFC Offensive Rookie of the Year.

Unfortunately, the New England rebuilding program took a nose dive, and 1972 was a lost year for the team. The offensive line fell apart, making life miserable for Jim. A midseason coaching change worsened things, and before the year was

out, general manager Bell was gone, too.

But Jim Plunkett never complained. He knew it would be rough and he was willing to stick with it. Quitting wasn't in his nature.

Those who knew Jim off the field believed he was even a bigger winner there. Bob Woolf, Jim's friend and legal adviser, represented many athletes, yet he considered Jim very special. "There was tremendous pressure on Jim from the time he joined the Patriots," Woolf said. "With all the attention and praise he's received, he's never changed a bit. He's as level-headed and unspoiled as ever."

When the Patriots win that Super Bowl some year in the future, Jim Plunkett will no doubt be there, still unspoiled.

Plagued by a weak offensive line in 1972, Jim is dropped by a Raider defender—but not before he threw the ball.

5

Jan Stenerud

There was a time not so long ago when professional football teams couldn't afford—or didn't feel they needed—a full-time kicking specialist. Kicking was a second job for a player best known at another position. Oakland's George Blanda was a quarterback long before he was valued for his kicking. Lou Groza, who became the greatest kicker of his generation for Cleveland in the 1950s and early '60s, was an All-Pro tackle in his prime. And Paul Hornung, the Golden Boy of Green Bay, was always best known for his running even though he also became a top kicker.

Many of these part-time kickers did their best booting when they weren't playing regularly at another position. Blanda and Groza were recognized as kickers after they passed their prime at their regular positions. Others—Hornung and Wayne Walker, a Detroit linebacker—gave up place-kicking because it demanded too much concentration. The pressure of doing justice to two jobs was a bit much to handle.

Then a few cagey coaches began to see the advantages of having a kicking specialist. The specialist could practice his special skill exclusively, could think about kicking during the entire season, and wouldn't get hurt while playing other positions.

At the same time that place-kickers became important, the styles of kicking began to change. The early kicking specialists were conventional-style, straightaway kickers. They stood directly behind the ball, facing the goal posts, and stepped straight into the ball, striking it with their toes.

Then in 1964, a strange phenomenon came to pro football. The Buffalo Bills of the American Football League drafted a place-kicker named Pete Gogolak from Cornell University. Gogolak had been born in Hungary and had grown up playing soccer. Owing to that game's tradition, he kicked a football from the side, soccer style.

When football people first saw Gogolak kick, they couldn't believe their eyes. He lined up to the left of the football, facing the right sideline, rather than the goal posts. At the snap, he would take one step and swing his right leg sideways, striking the ball with his instep instead of his toes. Surprisingly,

George Blanda kicks the ball with his toe . . .

within a year, he was one of the best kickers in all of football.

Gogolak was the pioneer, and soon other foreign-born kickers began drifting into pro football.

. . . while **Jan Stenerud boots it with the side of his foot.**

Today, there are almost as many sidewinders as straightaway kickers.

The pros and cons of each kicking style were debated for years. But there was one thing about kickers that was pretty well settled. When football people were asked who was the best kicker in the NFL, most answered without hesitation.

"Jan Stenerud."

Jan who? That's what everyone asked Kansas City Chief coach Hank Stram when he announced that Stenerud, a native Norwegian, would be the Chiefs' kicker for the 1967 season. But the wily Stram knew what he was doing.

He drafted Jan (pronounced *yahn*) out of Montana State University, then personally held the ball for his kicks during training camp. Even though Jan had a fine rookie season, Stram held a large kicking camp the following summer, inviting others to challenge Stenerud for his job. Stenerud easily beat back all the competition. Several kickers who were at that camp later became regular kickers with other NFL teams.

From the first time he jogged onto the field in a Kansas City uniform, Jan Stenerud was a game-breaker and a superstar. He was probably football's most accurate long-distance kicker, a threat to hit from anywhere inside the 50, and even from further out than that. Coming into the 1973 season, Stenerud had made 185 of 275 attempts, scoring on 67 percent of his tries. Many of his kicks were from long range, and many won ballgames for the Chiefs.

But how did a young Norwegian lad find fame and fortune in the American game of football? It wasn't easy, especially since Jan didn't even see a football game until he was 20 years old. He was born in 1943 in Fetsund, Norway, where American football was unknown. When Jan was born, World War II was raging and Norway was occupied by the Germans. Very few people were thinking about sports at all.

Fortunately, the occupation soon ended, and Jan grew up in a healthy, happy environment. "Like so many boys in Norway," Jan said years later, "I was skiing by the time I was two years old. And before long, I started taking small jumps. I liked that better, and have done more jumping than straight skiing ever since.

"Then when I was eight, I started to play our version of football. You call it soccer." Soccer is played with a round ball and players are forbidden to touch it with their hands. They must move the ball and pass it back and forth using their feet, knees, shoulders or head.

"Anyway, I was in organized soccer in Norway for ten years, so I did plenty of kicking. I was usually a forward, and I was best at making accurate passes [kicks] to the big goal scorer. I really enjoyed the game."

In 1962, Jan decided to visit his sister, who was already living in America. He stayed with her in Buffalo, New York, and in September of 1963, he saw his first football game—between the Buffalo Bills and the Kansas City Chiefs of the American

Football League. He sat with sportswriter Larry Felser of the *Buffalo Evening News.*

At one point the Bills' field goal unit came onto the field and Tommy Brooker got ready for a 31-yard try. "What's he doing now?" Stenerud asked.

"He's going to kick a field goal," Felser answered. "If he can kick the ball between those upright posts, the team gets three points."

Jan looked at the goal posts, then back to Brooker. "That shouldn't be too hard," he said seriously. "At least not for a soccer player."

Jan forgot football and soon entered Montana State University on a skiing scholarship. He was looking forward to ski jump competition in America. At Montana State he became champion intercollegiate jumper. He sometimes soared more than 300 feet (the length of a football field).

One day in the fall of 1964, Jan was working out for the ski season, hopping on one leg up the steps of the football stadium. This exercise, which he did every day, strengthened his legs for the landing impact of the ski jump. But on this day, Jan wandered down on the field after his exercises and found a football on the grass. He remembered the game he had seen in Buffalo a year earlier and decided to try kicking the ball at the uprights.

He made a depression in the grass 40 yards from the goal posts and set the ball up. He got set behind the ball and to the left, then took two quick steps and swung his leg through, soccer style. The ball soared on a line and cleared the uprights with room to spare. He tried again with the same results. Wearing tennis shoes and with no previous practice in his life, Jan Stenerud was doing something that other players couldn't do after five years of work.

Some of the football players were still in the stadium after their practice session. They watched Stenerud's amazing kicks and then quickly told coach Jim Sweeney about the Norwegian ski jumper with the powerful right leg. Sweeney found their stories hard to believe, but when he saw Jan in action he was soon convinced.

Sweeney made an appointment with Jan and invited him to come out for football the following year. There was only one game left in the current season, and Jan sat on the bench to observe the action. Sweeney warned him that American football was a tough game, but Jan didn't seem worried. After all, he was used to hitting the ground on skis after flying more than 100 yards through the air.

When the 1965 season opened Jan reported to the Montana State team as a field goal kicker. To take advantage of his new star, Sweeney used a new strategy. In college football, the goal posts are ten yards behind the goal. Yet anytime Montana State had the ball nearer than the 50-yard line on fourth down, Sweeney sent Stenerud in to try for a field goal. There was always a chance that Jan would make it, and if he didn't his kick would serve as a punt.

It didn't take long before the young kicker had a nationwide reputation. Montana State didn't have a strong team, and Jan was almost always booting for distance. He made only seven of fourteen attempts during the season, but they were from 27, 28, 36, 39, 41 and 59 yards out. His 59-yard boot set an intercollegiate record. Jan enjoyed his first year of college football, but he still thought he could do better.

There was just one problem. He was scheduled to graduate the following June. He cut down on the number of courses he was taking so that he could return for the 1966 fall semester. It was a good move. He had already been drafted as a "future" by Kansas City in the AFL and Atlanta in the NFL. But now he could play another college season and perfect his skills.

The Montana State attack was more effective in 1966, and Jan saw a lot of action. When the season ended, he had converted 49 of 52 extra points and boomed home 11 of 19 field goal attempts. But that's even better than it seems. Six of his attempts were from more than 40 yards, and on these he was acting more as a punter than a field goal kicker. On tries from less than 40 yards he made 11 of 13. In all, Jan scored 82 points, a new collegiate record, and he was chosen as the kicking specialist on the *Sporting News* All-America team.

Both Kansas City and Atlanta were eager to sign the powerful kicker. They knew how valuable his foot could be in the pros. Other scouts were impressed, too. A scout for the 49ers watched Jan one afternoon and said afterward, "Stenerud is already ten to twelve yards better than anyone in the NFL."

One kick stood out in everyone's mind. Jan was sent in to try a field goal from the Montana State 43. Jan stepped into the ball, and it sailed off the mark in a whistling, low curve. It kept rising and rising. The return man, stationed on the 20, began running backwards.

The ball hit on the chalk stripe right under the goal posts, ten yards behind the goal line. It had traveled 67 yards in the air. Although it was only a missed field goal in the record books, probably no kicker in the country could have booted the ball so far.

As soon as the 1966 season ended, both Kansas City and Atlanta began making offers to Stenerud. In fact, the Chiefs invited him for a tryout late that year. When Jan arrived on the field, coach Hank Stram approached the youngster and asked if he wanted to loosen up his leg. Kickers usually warm up by making short kicks, then increase the distance slowly. But Jan took a football, teed up the ball at the 40, and calmly booted it through the uprights. Then he repeated the process with the same results.

"OK, coach," he said. "I'm loose now. What do you want me to do?"

Stenerud approaches the ball at an angle, swings his
leg from the side and hits the ball with his instep.

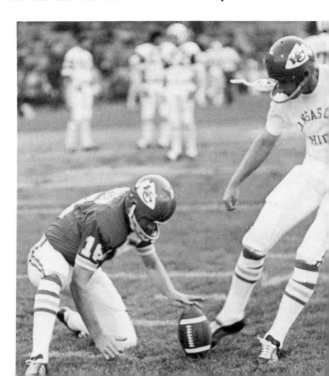

Stram was amazed. Tight end Fred Arbanas watched Jan's kicks, then ran over to Stram. "Coach," he said excitedly. "If we don't sign this kid, we'll be making the mistake of our lives."

Although the Chiefs didn't know it, Jan had already made up his mind: "I knew where I wanted to play five minutes after I met coach Stram. He was really impressive. Most people would just talk money and talk about the contract. Coach Stram talked about kicking, and he really knew what he was talking about. I knew then that he could help me and that he was the coach I wanted to play for."

Stram took a personal interest in Jan. A month before training camp began in 1967, Stram went out with his rookie kicker every day. The roly-poly coach did the holding, and Jan kicked as many as 50 balls. Stram's explanation was simple. "Heck, I didn't know anything about soccer-style kickers," he said. "How do you expect me to help him if he ever gets in a slump unless I know what he's doing?"

In his rookie season Jan established a permanent place for himself. He kicked 21 field goals and 45 extra points, leading the league in three-pointers and placing second in total scoring. In his very first professional game, he calmly booted a 54-yard field goal to help the Chiefs defeat the Houston Oilers.

But he wasn't completely satisfied. "It's part of a kicker's job to stay calm," Jan told an inter-

101

viewer. "He's got to produce when it counts, and it gets rather nerve-racking out there. But I've calmed down some already. And now that I have a year under my belt, the experience should make me that much better."

When the 1968 exhibition season opened, Jan became a genuine gamebreaker when he won two of the Chiefs' first three exhibition games. Then on September 12, he started the regular season by booting field goals from 27, 33, 26 and 32 yards out, to help the Chiefs to a 26–21 win over Houston. He was named Associated Press Offensive Player of the Week for the first time.

"Coach Stram and I stopped at Indiana State College on the way down here," Jan said. "That way, I got to practice on artificial turf and was able to adjust my kicking rhythm. That really helped."

At 6-foot-2 and 185 pounds, Jan wasn't big by football standards. Still, he was wiry and tough. And his kicking leg, the right one, was a marvel. Bermuda shorts that fit loosely on his left leg hardly fit at all on his right.

Jan's second season was no letdown. He had 30 field goals in 40 attempts and was second in the league scoring race to the Jets' Jim Turner. His 75 percent accuracy made him the most reliable kicker in the league.

Jan approached his specialized skill with the meticulous care of an artist. He knew just how much kicking his leg could take in the week before the game. No matter how well or how poorly he kicked in practice, Jan never booted the ball more than 35 times a day during training camp. He made 20 kicks a day early in the week before a game. Then, on Friday and Saturday he would kick just 10 or 15 times. Kicking a football puts tremendous strain on a kicker's leg, and Jan's routine was designed to make him well-practiced but not tired on the day of a game.

It's estimated that Jan and other soccer-style kickers could drive the ball about eight yards longer and 15 miles per hour faster on the average than straightaway kickers. When Jan kicked, the ball left the ground at about 90 miles per hour. It was important that he kick exactly the same way every time so that the precision timing between kicker and holder would not be thrown off.

The year before Jan arrived in Kansas City, the Chiefs had won the AFL championship and played in the first Super Bowl. They had been beaten badly by the Green Bay Packers and had vowed to come back to win.

In 1969 they seemed to be on their way again, and Stenerud was one big reason. On November 7, Jan entered the game with Buffalo in the first quarter and booted a 47-yard field goal. Four more times he trotted onto the field that afternoon and kicked three-pointers of 34, 37, 44 and 18 yards. He made five straight, and the Chiefs won easily.

The next week he kicked successfully from the

103

30 and 47 against San Diego. Against the Jets the following Sunday he booted field goals of 21 and 38 yards. Jan had kicked nine straight field goals without a miss. The NFL record, set by Lou Groza, was twelve.

Jan got only a single chance in each of the next two games, but they were easy ones of 14 and 16 yards. Then on December 7, against Buffalo once more, he had a chance to tie the record with his first kick.

When he came onto the field in the second period, the ball was resting on the Kansas City 45-yard line. The record-tying effort would be a kick of 52 yards. The odds were all against him.

Holder Len Dawson knelt down precisely seven yards behind the line. Jan was two yards beyond that and off at his customary angle to the left. The ball was snapped.

Dawson placed the ball down, spinning it so that the laces faced away from the kicker. Jan took two quick steps, planted his left heel and swung his right leg into the ball, hitting an inch-wide target on the pigskin. The ball soared toward the goal posts, climbing steadily, and passed easily between the uprights. Jan had tied the record with a mammoth 52-yard shot. His teammates congratulated him at the bench, and he smiled. He liked kicking the long ones, but he was thinking more about winning the game.

The Chiefs needed Jan that afternoon. He came

onto the field four more times and kicked three-pointers of 8, 47, 29 and 25 yards. Not only did he break the record with an amazing 16 straight field goals, but his kicking was directly responsible for another victory, as the Chiefs won 22–19.

Jan's statistics by the end of the Buffalo game were hard to believe. He had made 27 of 34 field goal attempts for a .784 average. He trailed Turner again in the scoring race, but there wasn't a more accurate kicker in all of football.

Kansas City finished a shade behind Oakland in the AFL West Division. But they got another chance to make the Super Bowl in a round-robin playoff. They beat the New York Jets, then beat the Raiders, to win the AFL title and enter the Super Bowl against the powerful Minnesota Vikings.

The Vikings were overwhelming favorites, since many fans still believed that NFL teams were better than those in the AFL. But one thing the experts didn't count on was the gamebreaking ability of Jan Stenerud.

The contest was scoreless until midway through the first period. Then Stenerud came on to try a field goal from the 48.

"No chance!" screamed the confident Vikings. But Jan fooled them. He booted the 48-yarder with ease and gave the Chiefs a 3–0 lead.

By the time the second period was half over, Jan had kicked two more, from 32 and 25 yards out. He gave his team a 9–0 lead and helped break

the Viking spirit. Two Chief touchdowns made the
final count 23–7. Jan's personal total of eleven
points (three field goals and two extra points) was
more than the entire Viking squad could muster.

"Their place-kicker was the Most Valuable
Player in this one," said Viking defensive end Carl
Eller after the game. "With him in there, the defense is under tremendous pressure. You know you
can't let them inside the 50 or Stenerud will do his
thing."

The game solidified Jan's reputation as the best
place-kicker in football. The next season, 1970, he
won his first AFC scoring title with 116 points. In
1971 he had another fine year but suffered one of
the biggest disappointments of his career.

Kansas City was playing the Miami Dolphins
in the first round of the playoffs. The score was tied
at 24-all with 31 seconds left. The Chiefs had the
ball at the Miami 24, and Jan came out to attempt
the winning field goal. For him, a 31-yard attempt
was hardly unusual.

The ball was placed down. His timing was perfect. The kick was away. All eyes were on the ball
as it sailed high and far. But at the last second it
dipped slightly to the right and missed the upright
by inches. Jan stared in disbelief, then left the field
with his head down. He waited for a chance to re-
deem himself, but it never came. In the second
overtime period, Miami's Garo Yepremian, another soccer-style kicker, ended football's longest

The sidelines in Kansas City are a long way from Jan's birthplace in Norway.

game with a 37-yard field goal. He did what Jan failed to do, and he was the hero.

At first Stenerud even talked about quitting. The Chiefs reminded him of all the games he'd won for them over the years and encouraged him to continue. After all, his missed field goal was only one of several missed opportunities for Kansas City that day.

A few weeks later Jan appeared in the Pro Bowl game and kicked four field goals. But he couldn't forget about the one he missed. "It'll probably be the most famous kick of all time, until someone misses a bigger one," he said. "Even if I kick a hundred field goals next year, this is going to stay with me."

Jan weathered the storm and came back strong in '72. His booming kicks hadn't changed, and neither had he. Still a happy, outgoing man, Jan Stenerud wouldn't forget the kick that failed, but he wouldn't let it beat him, either. He went on kicking the ball like no man before him.

Coach Hank Stram remembered the kicks Jan had made, not the one that got away. "Jan is an integral part of our team," the coach said. "He adds a new dimension to our offense. Whenever we get near midfield, we can score three points. There's no doubt in my mind that he's the greatest long-distance field goal kicker who ever played the game."

6

Bruce Taylor

One afternoon in the fall of 1969 the phone rang in the sports editor's office of a small Southern Connecticut newspaper. When the editor answered, a man with a deep, cultured voice introduced himself, then quickly came to the point.

"As a graduate of Boston University, I feel obligated to ask you to write something about Bruce Taylor," the man said.

"Bruce who?" the editor asked.

"Bruce Taylor. He's the best football player Boston U. ever had. We're trying to see that he gets some recognition, and I thought you might like to do a story on him."

The editor explained that his paper wasn't very

large and usually published news of the local community. But the caller was hard to convince. About a week later, he tried again.

"Listen," he said, "this Bruce Taylor had another great game last week. He only plays defense and runs back kicks, but he's our leading scorer. I'll tell you something, he's going to make a great pro someday."

The sports editor had never heard anything else about Bruce Taylor. Boston University was hardly a major football power, and Taylor was only a defensive player. He thanked the man for his information and promptly forgot about Taylor. It never crossed the editor's mind that someday he would be telling the Bruce Taylor story in a book called *Gamebreakers of the NFL.*

By the end of the 1970 season, football fans around the country had heard of Bruce Taylor. The pro scouts hadn't ignored his performances at Boston U., and he had been drafted in the first round by the San Francisco 49ers. Then he had about as great a rookie season in 1970 as a player could hope for. He started by winning the Most Valuable Collegian award in the College All-Star game. Then he earned a starting cornerback job with the 49ers and became the most feared punt returner in the league. At the end of the season he was named Defensive Rookie of the Year in the NFC. From out of nowhere, a new star had burst upon the football scene.

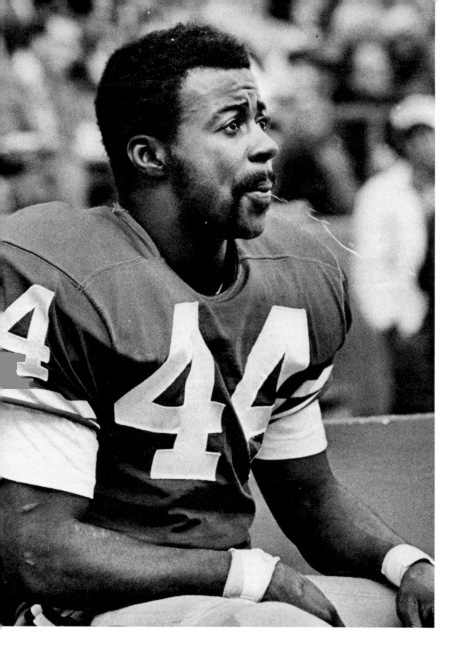

San Francisco's Bruce Taylor.

Bruce Lawrence Taylor was born in Perth Amboy, New Jersey, in May of 1948. By the time he reached high school, he was a star in three sports and was drafted by the Baltimore Orioles as an outfielder when he graduated.

But instead of taking the money and going into the Oriole organization, Bruce accepted a football scholarship and went to college at Boston University. There he became an immediate standout on a weak team. He received little attention outside of Boston—his team didn't play major football powers and even lost many of its games to weak competition. But Bruce worked quietly at his job, sharpening his skills as a defensive back and kick returner. He knew just where he wanted to go. At the same time, he dominated his team as perhaps no defensive back or punt returner ever has.

Taylor returned 24 punts during his senior season, and gained more than 500 yards. He averaged 21.4 yards per return. Fans were used to seeing his 6-foot, 180-pound body accelerate past the first wave of tackles, fake past the second wave, and then break into the clear and turn on the speed.

He scored six touchdowns that season to lead his team in scoring. Three came on punt returns, one on the return of a missed field goal, one on a pass interception and the other on his only offensive play from scrimmage, a 48-yard TD dash on an end-around play. A seventh touchdown—an 88-yard punt return—was called back on a penalty.

112

"Bruce always gave us that spark when we needed it most," said Boston U. coach Larry Naviaux. "He just took off with punts and kickoffs and put us in great field position. Much of the success the team had can be attributed directly to Bruce."

When Boston played Harvard, Harvard coach John Yovicsin ordered his punter to keep the ball away from Taylor at all costs. As a result, Harvard's punts were short and ineffective and led directly to a Boston victory.

The following week, when the Terriers met the University of Massachusetts, Taylor broke up a close game. He caught a field goal attempt four yards deep in the end zone, eluded two tacklers with a stutter-step at the 5, sprinted past five others, then picked up blockers and raced down the sideline for a 104-yard touchdown romp, the longest return in Terrier history.

He had a 50-yard kickoff return against Lafayette and a brilliant 24-yarder against Maine in which he single-handedly broke a half dozen tackles. Against Connecticut, he made a leaping interception at the 18 and took it back 82 yards on a dazzling, zigzagging broken field run. Later he broke a 45-yard punt return for another touchdown. His play led to a 37–21 Terrier upset. Connecticut coach John Toner predicted that Bruce Taylor would be "the first New England player drafted by the pros this year."

113

Bruce's own defensive coach, Ron Mitchell, thought an important aspect of Bruce's game was being ignored. "Everyone is so intent on watching Bruce return punts and kickoffs that they ignore his fine work at cornerback," Mitchell said. "Against Connecticut alone, he was credited with being involved in 16 tackles. He was all over the field. I can't figure out how he covers so much ground so fast. He has a nose for the football and always knows which way the play is going."

Before the season ended, Taylor's mind was already on pro football. Pro scouts had made special trips to see him play, and he knew he would be drafted early. He was named to the Little All-America team, then concentrated on getting his degree in history as he waited for the pro draft.

In the city of San Francisco, some 3,000 miles from Boston, the NFL's 49ers were having problems. They had won only four games in 1969, yet on paper they looked like they should be winners.

"We knew we had a good football team," said head coach Dick Nolan. "We attributed five of the losses directly to failures of our special teams—our kicking game and our kick-return game were lousy."

Nolan quickly cured half of the problem by trading experienced cornerback Kermit Alexander to Los Angeles for a good place-kicker, Bruce Gossett. Some fans thought Alexander was too good a player to give up. "I traded Alexander because I was confident we could get Tannen or Taylor in the draft," Nolan explained.

Steve Tannen was a highly publicized corner-back from Florida who later joined the New York Jets. Bruce Taylor was from Boston University—49er scouts had not overlooked him. When San Francisco's first pick came in the draft, both Tannen and Taylor were available.

"We picked Taylor," the coach said, "because he could serve a dual role as a return man as well as a cornerback. Tannen was strictly a corner-back."

When informed that San Francisco had picked him first, Bruce said, "It's a great honor to be a first-round choice. I'm looking forward to playing with the 49ers."

Then Bruce showed the quiet confidence that was his trademark. Although he hadn't yet made the team, he said, "Since the 49ers traded Kermit Alexander to make room for me, I'm sure I'll have every opportunity to play ball. It's a good feeling to go to a team that really wants you."

But before reporting to the 49ers' training camp for the 1970 season, Bruce stopped in Chicago to play in the College All-Star game against the world champion Kansas City Chiefs. Said Alex Agase, the All-Star defensive coach, "I've never seen a better corner back at this stage of his career than Bruce Taylor. He does everything well, and he's got a good football mind."

BRUCE TAYLOR

Taylor used the game to prove that the 49ers had made no mistake in drafting him. Although the Chiefs moved easily on the ground, they had a difficult time kicking and passing against the youngster from Boston University. In the first half he ran

Taylor takes the ball on a kickoff . . .

BRUCE TAYLOR

back one kickoff 33 yards, and had another 36-yard scamper called back by a clipping penalty. Each time, he eluded the Kansas City defenders brilliantly. Some observers even compared his running style to that of the great Gale Sayers.

. . . and heads for the goal.

In the second half he grabbed a Kansas City punt at the 12, weaved his way through the first wave of tacklers, faked past two more and almost broke away before getting trapped at the 40. It was a 28-yard return, once again giving the All-Stars good field position.

The Chiefs won the game 24–3. But the star of the All-Stars was obviously Bruce Taylor, and he won the College MVP award which had almost always been won by offensive players.

Taylor's runbacks weren't the only thing that attracted attention. Bruce also did a fine job of pass coverage against Kansas City receivers Otis Taylor, Frank Pitts and Gloster Richardson. Pitts made two catches on him, but the other two were blanked.

"They were all big," said Bruce after the game, "plus they had speed and moves. But I'm sure I can get used to covering them with no trouble. When I came to college I was a running back, and I didn't like it when they made me a defensive back. But now I love the intricacies of defense and I'm confident I can play the pro game."

Taylor finally reported to the 49er camp, intent on making the starting team. The first day he scrimmaged, coach Nolan assigned him to cover Gene Washington, the 49ers' All-Pro receiver.

"I guess they wanted to make sure I didn't get too cocky," Bruce said, smiling. "Gene showed me a thing or two right off the bat. He's got some fantastic moves and made me feel pretty bad. But it also reminded me that I'd have to work really hard to learn the receivers and the best way to play them."

By playing in the All-Star game, Taylor missed three weeks of training camp. Shortly after reporting, he suffered a muscle pull that put him even farther behind. He wasn't at full strength until the final two exhibition games, against Los Angeles and Oakland. He did so well in those contests, though, that Nolan named him as a starter for the first regular-season game against Washington. Taylor had achieved his first goal.

"I learned a lot in those exhibitions," Bruce said. "I'm sorry I didn't play in all of them. But there are some things I know I won't do again. When we played the Raiders, Warren Wells beat me for a touchdown simply because I took my eyes off him and looked back at the ball. You don't do that. To put it into basics, you must stay with the receiver, and these guys have a lot of ways to shake you.

"I won't be completely satisfied until I have the same feeling I always had in college," he continued. "Then I felt that I could stop anybody or anything. I've sensed the feeling coming back in the last couple of weeks, but the only way I'll get it all is to keep playing and working. That's why I'm so happy that coach Nolan picked me to start."

Once the season began, there was no looking

back. With veterans Jim Johnson and Roosevelt Taylor constantly helping and instructing the rookie, Bruce held up under the early season pressure. Johnson, who played regularly at the other corner, was an All-Pro. Opposing quarterbacks avoided throwing into his zone. Instead, they threw to Taylor's side, and Bruce had some very busy afternoons of football. He was burned a few times, but more often than not he did his job.

As a punt returner, he needed help and advice from no one. Excelling from the start at one of football's more demanding specialties, he electrified the fans week after week with his dazzle on returns. He could squirm through the smallest hole, fake defenders off their feet and use blazing speed to outrun his frustrated pursuers. In a matter of weeks he had given the 49ers what they had been lacking in the past, a kick-return game.

The team was winning. By the time they had played eight games, the 49ers were on top of the NFC's Western Division with a 6–1–1 mark. Already they had won more games than in 1969. With a revitalized offense led by John Brodie and a solid, maturing defense, San Francisco was tough to beat. Bruce Gossett was a dependable place-kicker, and Bruce Taylor made the kick-return game one of the most feared in the entire NFL.

Coming into the ninth game against the Houston Oilers, Taylor had a 13.3-yard punt return average, best in the NFC. His return yardage was even more impressive because he rarely called for a fair catch. He preferred to chance a run, even with four or five defensive players bearing down on him. He was often dropped instantly for no gain, but he sometimes squirmed away from his pursuers and left them behind.

When asked about his reluctance to signal for a fair catch, Bruce answered quickly, "Anyone can call for a fair catch. They wanted someone to run the ball back, and that's my job—running it."

Then Taylor took the field against the Oilers. Six times he returned punts that day, and he gained a total of 133 yards, an average of 22 yards a return. Two of the runbacks led directly to 49er scores, and another return of 31 yards was called back by a penalty. His yardage in that game alone surpassed the season-long total of the 49er punt returners in 1969. When the game was over, San Francisco had a 30–20 victory, and Bruce Taylor was given the game ball for his contribution.

"It's the greatest thing that ever happened to me," he said afterward. Then he looked at his smiling teammates. "No, the second greatest. The greatest was being drafted by the 49ers in the first round."

Then Bruce explained his return technique to the cluster of reporters gathered around his locker. "First I watch the ball leave the kicker's foot so I'll know where it's coming. Then I look for the action in the line [of charging defenders], and I don't look

121

back at the ball until I'm almost ready to grab it. That way, I can usually tell where there's going to be room to run."

Whatever he was doing, it was the right thing. When the 1970 season ended, Taylor was leading the NFC with an average of 12 yards gained per punt return. He had carried back 43 kicks (the second highest number of returns ever) for 516 yards. He had called for a fair catch only ten times. In contrast, Ed Podolak, who led the AFC with a 13.5-yard average, ran back only 23 punts and called for 21 fair catches.

In addition, Bruce made three interceptions and scored his only touchdown on a 92-yard return of a missed field goal. His longest punt return covered 76 yards, while he almost broke several others for scores.

The 49ers finished with a 10–3–1 record to edge the Rams for the divisional title and a place in the playoffs. It was the first time the 49ers had ever made the playoffs, and they were already thinking ahead to the Super Bowl.

On December 27, they met the rough, tough Minnesota Vikings at Kezar Stadium in San Francisco. It was not a good day for most of the 49ers. The 49er offense was punished all afternoon by the rugged Minnesota defense. Luckily, the 49ers also held the Vikings. The only man the Vikings couldn't contain was Bruce Taylor. Taylor danced

BRUCE TAYLOR

past the Minnesota tacklers with two brilliant punt returns of 20 and 30 yards. Both times the 49ers marched in to score. A Gossett field goal settled the issue, giving the 49ers a 17–14 victory.

Then the 49ers played the Dallas Cowboys for the NFC title and a place in the Super Bowl. Before

Taylor (44) is the 49ers' last hope to catch Cowboy running back Duane Thomas in the 1971 NFC championship game.

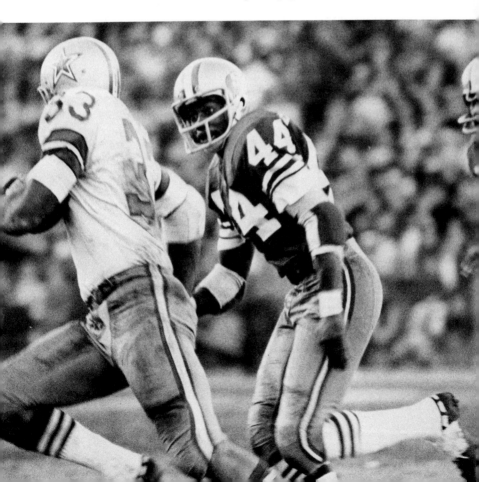

the game Cowboy scout Ermal Allen talked about San Francisco's young cornerback. "No doubt about it, Bruce Taylor won the Minnesota game for the 49ers," Allen said. "Both his punt returns were brilliant, and both led to touchdowns. We're going to be very careful with him on Sunday."

It was quite a tribute to the rookie, and the Cowboys made good on Allen's promise. Dallas kicker Ron Widby booted high and away from Bruce, and Taylor was unable to get off a good return. Two Dallas interceptions of John Brodie passes gave the Cowboys the advantage, and they won 17–10, ending the season for San Francisco.

For Bruce it had been quite a year. Soon after the game, he learned he had been voted the NFC's Defensive Rookie of the Year. The confident youngster had exceeded even his own expectations.

"He's a really outstanding cornerback," said coach Nolan. "And he's the type of guy who plays better in clutch situations and in big games. He performs under pressure, and that's always the mark of a great player."

Taylor reported the next year with the same quiet confidence and the added poise of a veteran. When someone mentioned another rookie cornerback who might challenge him for a job, Bruce replied, "I'll tell you something. The guy isn't going to play in front of me. I earned this spot, and I don't intend to give it up for a long time."

Bruce's 1971 season would have been more

than adequate for most players, but it was a bit of a disappointment for him. He was now a respected cornerback, and fewer passes were thrown in his direction. Still, he picked off three passes, returning them for a total of 68 yards. More disappointing was his record for punt returns. By midseason he was averaging only 4.6 yards a return and had called for six fair catches.

"I'm a marked man," he told newsmen, with a trace of a smile. "Other teams know me now and they know the threat of our punt return unit, so they've been releasing sooner at the line and kicking away from me. A lot of them kick out of bounds, and the others are kicking high even if it means a shorter punt. But don't worry, I'll pop one before the season ends."

Things did get somewhat better. Despite nagging ankle injuries Taylor increased his return average to 6.9 yards, good for sixth place in the NFC. The 49ers finished at 9–5 and entered the playoffs again. They won their first game, 24–20, over Washington, but Taylor was injured. He was at less than full speed the next week when the 49ers bowed to Dallas for the second straight year.

The 49ers were in the thick of battle again in '72, winning their division title before being toppled in the playoffs. Playing opposite all-pro cornerback Jimmy Johnson, Bruce was under continuous pressure—rival quarterbacks were reluctant to throw to Johnson's side so threw to Bruce's instead.

But if Bruce Taylor has his way, NFL signalcallers will soon be hesitant to throw at either San Francisco cornerback.

"The minute you begin doubting your ability to perform," he once said, "it's time to start thinking about retirement."

For Bruce Taylor, that time was still a long way off.

7

Willie Lanier

"I guess I was always a hard hitter," Said Willie Lanier, talking about his early football days at Maggie Walker High in Richmond, Virginia. "I remember that in three of the first five games I played as a sophomore, an opposing player went out with a bad injury, a broken bone or separated shoulder, something like that. I was called a dirty ballplayer then, but I wasn't. As a matter of fact, I've never taken a cheap shot at a guy in my life.

"But I'll tell you this. I went out of my way to be a big hitter in high school and in college, too. I wanted to play pro ball, and I was pretty sure that the pro coaches liked big hitters. You know something? I was right."

Sitting on a sofa, his 6-foot-1, 245-pound frame

127

motionless, Willie Lanier didn't look like a violent man. Yet Kansas City's brilliant middle linebacker was one of the hardest hitters in a sport that demands hard hitters. And he was considered one of the two or three best linebackers in the NFL, in a class with Dick Butkus, Tommy Nobis, Mike Lucci and Mike Curtis.

Although he was known to his teammates as "Bear," or "Contact," Willie was sometimes puzzled by the violent game in which he excelled. "Sometimes I ask myself why I have to hit so hard," he said. "There's no answer as far as I can see. Here I am, a grown man with a family, but my livelihood means I have to hit people as hard as I can. It's the only way I've ever played the game.

"But it doesn't keep me from wondering if such conduct is necessary in the framework of life. And I ask myself how long a man can take the kind of punishment that football brings on. Don't forget, the hitter feels the blow almost as much as the guy he's hitting."

Just who was this sensitive, thinking man who had risen to the top of his profession in just six years? The facts tell part of the story. He was a middle linebacker, one of the keys to a football defense, and a position that requires a man to be

Kansas City linebacker Willie Lanier.

quick, strong, tough, mobile and intelligent. In 1971, Willie Lanier was All-Pro—the best at this difficult position in the entire NFL. In addition, Willie had team responsibilities, serving as captain of one of the top defensive units in pro football.

Willie Lanier was also a black man—the first black to become a top middle linebacker. Middle backers have traditionally been white, just as quarterbacks have been white. Although black men have become stars in pro football, few have had the chance to excel at these leadership positions.

Lanier was proud of his excellence: "Some people have called me the 'black Dick Butkus.' That kind of statement annoys me, because it sets up a double standard for rating football players. You can't compare players along lines of race or color. Just because our great kicker, Jan Stenerud, is from Norway, you don't hear other kickers referred to as American Jan Steneruds. It just isn't done."

Willie wanted to be compared to others on his merits, and many of his opponents considered him the best, regardless of color. "Lanier is the best linebacker I've ever played against," said Washington running back Larry Brown. "It's a shame that he doesn't get more publicity. He deserves it."

Larry Csonka, the fierce fullback of the Miami Dolphins, who earned his living powering his way past middle linebackers, said, "In one game Willie hit me so hard that I came out with double vision. It's not easy running against a grizzly bear. But

130

Willie goes one step further. He's a smart grizzly bear. Lanier against power football is what defense is all about."

Perhaps the ultimate compliment came from Lanier's teammate Buck Buchanan. Buck was a 286-pound All-Pro defensive tackle. Obviously, he could take care of himself. Yet Buchanan said, "I'll keep playing this game as long as Willie is playing behind me. But when he quits playing, that'll be the end of my career, too."

Buchanan went on to explain how Willie Lanier made the job of the defensive end so much easier. "Willie not only cuts off sweeps, he cuts off everything," said Buck. "He just stops the whole team."

But above all, Willie Lanier was a gamebreaker. For example, he was named NFL Defensive Player of the Week for his performance in Kansas City's 16–3 victory over Denver in 1971. In that game, Lanier made eight unassisted tackles, assisted on two more, recovered a fumble and broke up a key pass play early in the game. These are not record-breaking statistics, but nearly all of Willie's plays came at important points in the game.

"Every time Denver seemed to get something going, Lanier was there to stop them," said one writer. "It seemed to me that he made forty tackles. I noticed by the second half that the Broncos seemed to be running their plays away from number 63, not at him. He really dominated the game on defense."

WILLIE LANIER

Willie Edward Lanier was born in 1945, in Clover, Virginia. His family moved to Richmond when Willie was still a toddler. His parents worked very hard, Mr. Lanier as a shipping clerk for an electrical supply company, and Mrs. Lanier as a beautician. So Willie, his two older brothers and younger sister had a fairly comfortable life.

"They're good people," Willie said of his parents. "They were very religious and strict, stressing the difference between right and wrong, but they never interfered with our personal freedom. They let us grow and develop as individuals."

Robert, Jr., and Richard, Willie's older brothers, were the first of the football-playing Laniers. Both were good college players, and Richard once tried out with the Washington Redskins as a defensive back. But Willie was the one headed for a pro career.

As a 200-pound guard and linebacker at Maggie Walker High, Willie was a vicious hitter. His team lost only three games in four years and went unbeaten when he was a senior. But an all-black school in the South didn't attract many scouts from big football colleges. Willie got offers from some predominantly black colleges, but not from the one he wanted to attend.

"I knew that I had to go to a fairly well known football school to attract the attention of the pros," Willie explained. "I wanted Morgan State for that reason. So I called the coach, Earl Banks, and

132

offered my services. I told him I needed a scholarship in return. It was something of a long shot, but it worked out. I got a partial scholarship and a student loan. Then I took some odd jobs to earn the rest. It wasn't easy, but I went to the school I wanted."

Morgan State had a tough schedule against other predominantly black colleges. Willie played with and against talented football players, including many future professionals. He helped his Morgan State team to 18 straight wins in his final two years, then sat back and waited for the pro draft of 1967.

The Kansas City Chiefs had two second-round choices that year, and the Chiefs used them to pick Willie and Jim Lynch, a linebacker from Notre Dame. It soon became clear that the two rookies would be competing for the same job—middle linebacker.

"I was well aware that there had never been a black starting middle linebacker," Willie said. "Maybe that made me work a little harder, I don't know. I just wanted to play pro ball and play the best way I could."

Lanier and Lynch switched between middle and outside linebacker during the exhibitions and the early games of the season. Then coach Hank Stram made his choice.

"Either Lynch or Lanier could have played in the middle," said Stram. "Both are intelligent foot-

Lanier smacks down the Redskins' Larry Brown, causing a fumble.

ball players with good physical assets. But Willie is bigger than Jim, and that's what determined my choice. We'd had trouble in the past with people running up the middle on us, and I knew that wouldn't happen with Willie there."

Lynch went on to become a great outside linebacker, and many observers considered the Chiefs' Lanier, Lynch and All-Pro Bobby Bell the best linebacking trio in the league.

Willie had won his starting position, but he had a lot to learn about the pro game. "It wasn't easy," he said. "I found that the pro defenses were much more complex, especially in the area of pass coverage. In college we had no special pass coverage plans. We played a simple 4–4 defense, and most of the teams stayed on the ground."

By the time the Chiefs met San Diego in the fourth game of the 1967 season, rookie Lanier had learned the defensive formations and was beginning to "read" offensive patterns and adjust accordingly. His coverage on runs was good, and his pass coverage was improving rapidly.

Then disaster struck. Willie later explained what happened: "I had developed a habit that went way back to high school. I would hit a ball-carrier head first, instead of with my shoulders. By driving my head right into a runner's belly, I thought I could slow him up more and make him think twice about running at me again. I would sort of lock my neck when I did it so that I wouldn't hurt myself or get a whiplash type of injury.

"It worked pretty well. So I didn't even think when I tried it against San Diego that day. I dove at their fullback, Brad Hubbert. I was in midair and unable to change direction. Hubbert brought his knee up at the last minute and made contact with my head. Bam!"

After the game, Willie began getting headaches and feeling dizzy. Then he developed double vision. He continued to play, but two weeks later collapsed in a game against Denver. He was carried from the field.

"I woke up in the hospital and thought I was dying," he recalled. "I had a brain concussion from when I hit Hubbert, and it had recurred. The doctors told me I could play again in a few weeks, but said the double vision might linger for a month or two. I tried to play in our tenth game, but the double vision returned. I was through for the season."

Willie feared that his career might be over. His wife was expecting a baby at the time, and he wondered how he would support his family. The injury couldn't have occurred at a worse time. Then he remembered that baseball star Frank Robinson had suffered a similar injury and had double vision, too. But Robinson got well and continued to play great baseball. This gave Willie hope.

In time, the double vision went away. He had a checkup at the famous Mayo Clinic before the 1968 season and was found to be in perfect health. Willie reported to training camp free of any lingering fears.

"I was still a hitter," he said, smiling. "But I had changed my tactics. I now used my shoulders instead of my head. That's the part of the body that should be used to hit with. It's made me a better tackler. Whenever I talk to young football players, I always advise them to use their head for thinking and their shoulders for tackling. I'd never teach a kid to tackle with his head. I was lucky to get away with it for so long."

Although Willie remained a vicious tackler, he said that the hardest hit he ever made was way back in high school. "I can't forget the time I hit Leroy Keyes [later with the Philadelphia Eagles] in one of our high school games. He was already a star runner and I was playing linebacker.

"He was running a sweep and I got an angle on him from the other side of the field. I hit him just as he started making his cut. I don't think I ever hit anyone harder. When I got off him, he said, 'Where did you come from?' Somehow he finished the first half, but I didn't see him again in the second half. When we see each other today, we still talk about that play."

The Chiefs remember another memorable tackle. They were playing the Oakland Raiders in the 1969 AFL championship game. On one play Raider fullback Hewritt Dixon came steaming through the line. Suddenly he met Willie Lanier.

"It wasn't much," Dixon recalled later. "Half of me landed in one place and the rest of me in another place. Then I pulled myself together and went on, trying to forget that a mountain had fallen on me."

Eyewitnesses say that Willie's tackle fired up the Chiefs, who went on to whip Oakland, 17–7, and win a place in Super Bowl IV against the tough Minnesota Vikings.

Before the big game Willie explained his job. "Minnesota is a strong inside rushing team," he said. "Any time a team runs inside, the middle linebacker has to be extra aware of his responsibilities. But let's face it, playing defense against a strong running attack brings it down to the meat of the game itself. It's man to man. No matter how you look at it, it still comes down to that."

The game pattern developed right from the start. The Vikings' tough quarterback, Joe Kapp, tried to establish his running game right away, sending big backs Dave Osborne and Bill Brown smashing through the middle of the Kansas City line. But with Lanier directing and spearheading the Kansas City defense, the Viking runners couldn't gain and their running attack faltered. The Chiefs took over, and three Jan Stenerud field goals made it 9–0 midway through the second period. Then Chief halfback Mike Garrett scored a touchdown, and it was 16–0 at the half.

Both teams scored a third-period touchdown,

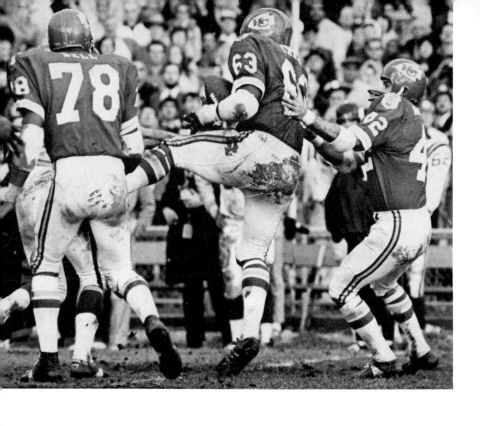

making the score 23–7. Now the Vikings were desperate to catch up, and the Chief defense had a picnic. Three interceptions, one by Lanier, ended Minnesota's hopes. The Chiefs were Super Bowl champions.

By this time, Willie was beginning to get some of the recognition his fierce play deserved. A few weeks after the Super Bowl he played in the pro All-Star game. After the 1970 season, he was named the All-AFC middle linebacker in three different polls. And in the Players' Association poll he was chosen the outstanding linebacker of 1970 in the whole NFL. Many consider this the ultimate honor for a pro player.

Willie refused to compare himself to other great middle linebackers. "There's no way you can make a true comparison unless all 26 teams have the same defenses and cover passes in the same way," he said. "One team might use its middle linebacker differently than another. For instance, on pass coverage, Mike Curtis [of Baltimore] drops back into the deep hook area every time and becomes part of their zone defense. We have a different system. So comparisons aren't so easy."

In 1971, Willie was off and hitting. He seemed quicker than ever. He was immovable on straight-ahead plays and was getting over to stop sweeps.

In the 1970 Super Bowl, Lanier intercepts a Viking pass (top) and heads for the goal. The Chiefs won 23–7.

141

On pass coverage, no linebacker in the league seemed to be in more places at once. He was everywhere, intimidating quarterbacks and racking up pass receivers with a vengeance.

By the time the season ended, Kansas City had won its division title with a 10–3–1 record and was headed for the playoffs once more. And this season, the newspaper polls named Willie Lanier the best middle linebacker not only in the AFC, but in the whole league. He had had a marvelous season.

"I don't really know if I can ever have a better season than I did this year," he said. "You know, even a football player has limits on his physical abilities. He reaches a peak and that's it. I don't know if it's possible for me to surpass what I did this season. I certainly approach every year with the idea of improving my performance. And you always improve from a mental standpoint—you learn more. There's no substitute for experience. But physically speaking, I think I did it all in '71."

One of Willie's big goals was to be on a second Super Bowl winner. He was disappointed in 1971 when the Chiefs lost a heartbreaker to Miami in the playoffs. It was the longest game ever played (two overtimes), and the Chiefs blew a 24–17 lead, losing 27–24 on Garo Yepremian's 37-yard field goal in the second extra period. But Lanier took the loss philosophically.

"I'm well aware of the importance of winning," Willie said after the game. "But I can't say I didn't

Willie (63) helps bring down Dolphin ball-carrier Larry Csonka.

enjoy playing in the game for its sheer competitiveness and suspense. An athlete should get some enjoyment from the game itself, not only from winning. Don't forget, I can look back for a long time and savor this one. I was in the longest game ever played, and I'll never forget it. Few people ever have an experience like that."

Willie was just as philosophical about his future. "In recent years, I've been giving more thought to developing a slightly different technique," he said. "You know, a little more finesse. The big hitting is something you can't do for 20 some-odd games. If it was just 14 games, then maybe. But if you continue to try to overpower everyone, the injuries begin to sneak up on you and you burn yourself out.

"I'm not interested in setting any records for longevity in this league. Maybe two or three more years will be enough. I've achieved most of my goals now, and I don't think I'd want to be doing this kind of thing when I'm over 30. I've got a wife and family to think about."

Willie was already a licensed realtor, had done some television work and studied to be a stockbroker. But for the time being, Willie Lanier was still a football player, stopping ball-carriers and intercepting passes. And he was the on-the-field brain behind the complex Kansas City defense.

As long as he played, he would make a big difference to the Chiefs with his talent and competitive spirit. An illustration of his attitude occurred in a 1969 playoff game against the New York Jets. The Chiefs had a slim lead in the fourth quarter when the Jets marched to a first down on the one-yard line. Kansas City cornerback Emmitt Thomas takes up the story from there.

"Willie became almost hysterical. He was crying and screaming. He started running up and down the defensive line begging us to stop the Jets. He said we'd worked like dogs since July and couldn't throw everything away now. There were tears running down his face.

"When the Jets came up to the line, Willie yelled, 'Dammit, they're not going to score on us!' Next thing we knew, we were all saying it and we just kept saying it, over and over."

Namath sent Matt Snell over the right side of the line. No gain. Then he sent Bill Mathis into the left side. No gain again. Then he rolled out to pass. Incomplete. The Jets had to settle for a field goal and the Chiefs went on to win, taking an important step toward the Super Bowl.

In that brief moment on the goal line, Willie's competitive spirit and leadership surfaced at once. He believed, and he made his teammates believe—helping to win another big game. Once again Willie Lanier had been a gamebreaker.

Index

Page numbers in italics refer to photographs.

INDEX

INDEX

INDEX

INDEX

151